Unleash, Unlearn, and Enliven

Unleash, Unlearn, and Enliven

Seven Micro-Practices to
Engage Your Somatic Wisdom

by Cristy De La Cruz

Published by
We Defy Definition

A division of DLC Solutions LLC

*Edited by Kay Grey * https://www.kaygrey.com/*

*Cover design by Natalya Kolosowsky * https://www.natalyakolosowsky.com/*

*Cover art by Heather Kusmider * https://heatherkusmider.wixsite.com/artwork*

Library of Congress Cataloguing-in Publication Data

Name: De La Cruz, Cristy Ann, 1974-author.
Title: Unleash, Unlearn, and Enliven: Seven Micro-practices to Engage Your Somatic Wisdom

ISBN: 979-8-9850-286-1-4 (eBook)
ISBN: 979-8-9850-286-2-1 (Paperback)
Subjects: somatics, neurodiversity, psychology, wellness, ADHD, bicultural people, mental health, depression

Dedicated to my family and to my ancestors,

particularly to my grandparents

who have passed from this earth,

without whom none of this would be possible.

Do I contradict myself?

Very well then I contradict myself,

(I am large, I contain multitudes.)

-WALT WHITMAN, EXCERPT OF SONG OF MYSELF, 51

~ Contents ~

Prologue   xi

Introduction   1

Part I: Unleash   7

Part II: Unlearn   57

Part III: Enliven   69

Part IV: Evolve   127

Connect   133

Acknowledgements   135

End Notes and References   137

Prologue

I inhaled sharply and searched my manager's eyes for some further explanation about the news she had just shared. I felt a weight on my chest and a simultaneous drop in my belly as though I had just been delivered to the bottom floor by an elevator with too swift a pulley, in need of repair. But her eyes wouldn't meet mine and instead dropped in front of her toward a copy of the letter she had pushed toward me upon sitting down with her and the Human Resources representative.

I searched the HR rep's glassy smile and poker face as I explained, "But I have so much left to DO here…" and then my voice trailed off as the news started to sink in. No. I had no work left to do here. A chilly bite in the air grabbed me and I shuddered. Cold, despite a warm room. I was being frozen, halted from the position where I had stirred up doubt and exposed land mines beneath an orderly surface.

"Inability to follow leadership direction" echoed in my mind, reverberating and familiar. Another phrase issued: "unprofessional behavior." This was a sharp slap, waking me up to what I was doing in this room after a long Monday of meetings.

I could not argue with their justifications for ending my contract. The Friday before this meeting I had written an email to my manager, admitting a professional gaffe I'd made, realizing I had caused unnecessary stress for a colleague. In it I had confessed that I struggle with a disability related to variable attention, not naming it specifically, but explaining how it can factor into my performance at work. I remember how much relief I'd felt in writing the email and finally sending it, coming out from hiding at last. My journal from that day recalled *"when we stop running from who we are, we can bring forth so much more beauty and strength to our work."*

It nearly made me laugh in this meeting, remembering that message with no response, no acknowledgement of being read. I had ignored the advice I'd accepted in sixteen years since receiving the official diagnosis. I was advised not to disclose a hidden disability unless it was truly necessary.

Therein lies the struggle: **when is disclosure necessary?** Is it when we suspect we are about to be fired? Is it when we realize that the busy conference room next to our office cubicle is presenting more problems than we anticipated with focusing on work? Is it when we realize that a jealous colleague has filed an anonymous complaint alleging something we could not have done?

Or do we disclose when carrying the mask feels too heavy? We long to finally be ourselves rather than pretending. It's just too exhausting to keep the shields up, to conform to the ways we are supposed to act in this setting. Authenticity is in vogue these days, isn't it?

Oh, but there are caveats. Only those that aren't dependent on this job as the main income source for their family can live out loud. Sheesh. I misunderstood. Can I take it back? Can I delete the confession from my manager's inbox and pretend the last week never happened? It was my first official termination, and I didn't expect it to hurt like a betrayal.

My work there was done. But the real work, the deep excavation to understand myself and truly come to terms with my neurodiversity was just beginning.

Introduction

Hidden in Plain Sight

Do you ever feel like you are wearing a disguise in your daily life? Or that you must don a virtual suit of armor that feels too heavy most days?

Maybe you view the world with a different kind of awareness that most people do not have? Your filter doesn't screen out certain details that others simply ignore. You are masking something about yourself that you suspect others may not understand. And you feel driven in a way that does not always make sense even to you.

You enjoy relative success in your career. However, you feel as though you are not living up to some elusive potential. You may have been told this so many times at school or at work that you internalized it. You may feel stuck in an area of your life. You are not satisfied with the advice from self-help books that ignore the effects of ableism and racism on your psyche. You are not alone. Your struggle is real, and it is valid.

What You Will Learn

Whatever brought you here, I know you have amazing and deep wisdom within you. The stories and practices in this book are meant to open a window into new ways to see yourself as you live with greater wholeness. My hope is that what I share will help you have more compassion for yourself. As you accept all parts of yourself and embrace those facets that may have felt alienated or relegated to the shadows, you will feel greater freedom and ease. You will have more courage to expand as you were meant to do. Though the fears may still be there, you will face them with greater resilience and equanimity.

Who is Cristy and How is She Qualified to Help?

You might be thinking to yourself, "All this sounds great, Cristy. But who are you and why should I listen to you?" I am so glad you asked. You are a skeptic! I am too.

My sensitivity to my own and others' emotions reflects internal wiring that I now describe as neurodiverse[1], though that remained a mystery until I was almost thirty. As an undergraduate, I studied psychobiology, which means I approach these topics from a multi-disciplinary, evidence-based framework. The phrase "research is me search" probably sums it up. Independently, I have read everything I can about the neuroscience of resilience and well-being for over sixteen years. But my personal desire to know and heal myself and others with higher-than-average sensitivity drives my obsessive focus on practical solutions to reduce suffering.

After a dozen years in the clinical research profession, I began to see how much it costs personally and societally when we do not proactively manage our wellness. I became a certified yoga teacher during my career "gap year" after leaving a high-pressure role in the medical device field. I learned meditation and self-awareness through somatic and body-based practices, and many of these techniques are the basis for the micro-practices described in the book. My conclusion after decades of academic and personal studies is that we are all our own best personal "laboratories" for discovery. To live happy and fulfilled lives we must find our way by tuning into deep soul wisdom and intuition, accessed through the body. As a coach for individuals and a facilitator for teams, I help people develop their own blend of practices to integrate learning and growth.

[1] Neurodiversity is a term first put forth by sociologist Judy Singer. It typically includes ADHD, autism, bipolar, dyslexia, or other "diagnoses" which may encompass qualities that include higher than average sensitivity in the nervous system.

Getting The Most from This Book

This journey reflects my lessons learned and practices that can help you embrace your glorious and multi-faceted identity. There are invitations that will ask you to think and write about your own experiences. There are micro-practices that will invite you to act in a physical or somatic way. Even if you read the entire book before exploring the invitations, I encourage you to come back and try each one for at least a week (or preferably a month) as an experiment. There are blank spaces throughout the book where you can write responses if you wish.

Some micro-practice invitations will feel easy and natural to incorporate into your life. Others may challenge you, and you may feel resistance to doing them. Pay special attention to those that you really do not want to do. If you keep a journal, make some notes about what feels "sticky" or difficult. This may be where you face an edge that is beckoning you to grow.

If you decide to make a deep commitment to your growth, try to devote a few minutes daily, or at least a few times per week, for a month or more before you "layer on" the next one. Habit change literature indicates that focusing on only one new practice or habit at a time is ideal until it feels easy. In all cases, be gentle with yourself. Certain practices may call out to us because they are what our deepest selves need to heal. This order can be different because we are unique. If your experiences with these practices do not match current needs, allow your inner wisdom and intuition to guide this path and modify accordingly.

If you can work through the invitations with a friend, mentor/coach, or with a small group, this can be especially beneficial. Having our experiences witnessed and validated by companions with similar challenges can help us see that while our journeys are unique, feeling "othered" is painful to all. Receiving witness and kindness from a trusted circle or mentor gives us an extra layer of support when difficult emotions inevitably arise.

You may uncover grief, anger, or sadness when it comes to rediscovering parts of yourself that may have been shut down. These emotions are a normal part of breaking through to deeper layers of your being. I find that releasing them through body-based practices helps us let go of the grip any old stories may have had over us or may still have. By freeing up this energy that may have "contained" those emotions and kept them at bay, we open ourselves to transformation.

If there is a part of yourself that feels vulnerable or fragile or not ready to be brought into the light, know that this is a process. You control the timeline. The emotional array that comes up will help build your resilience and compassion for others as well. We are so seldom alone in this work, though our culture has not necessarily made space for this growth.

If there is unhealed trauma in your past that comes up during this process, do your best to stay with your body and strong feelings that arise. Don't be afraid to reach out for professional support. I have taken this route numerous times. It saved my life at the time when depression had numbed me in a way that connecting with a compassionate witness was required.

If you are drawn to the work of uncovering your hidden identities, there is a good chance you are ready to express more of who you are in the world. This book is a starting point and can be used in conjunction with other modalities of support. You have had to navigate challenges in your life before. Many of the coping mechanisms you have developed might be helpful. Others may be less helpful if they developed when you were young and before you had developed greater capacity in your brain and nervous system to respond with discernment rather than over-react to emotional stimuli.

A Map of the Territory

Part I of this book begins with an exploration of identity and identities more broadly. Using myself as an example, I will unpack the search for our "selfhood" and invite you to ask questions to reflect on who you are. I explain why we often learn to hide and how this can be a useful adaptive function.

Since I call upon energetics and somatics as tools you can use for greater self-awareness and self-acceptance, I may touch on concepts that are new to you. I will explain why I include each suggestion using research and my lived experience to help anchor the ideas.

Part II is about Unlearning. It is about de-conditioning the cultural expectations we learned as young people. If you are like me, you learned to lie and hide to "protect" yourself and protect others' feelings. Once you understand why this was an adaptive strategy, it becomes easier to forgive yourself and reclaim your internal sovereignty.

Part III contains a series of seven micro-practices that have helped me to embrace and embody my internal identities with self-compassion and love. While not all your identities are ready to be shared with every person in your life, showing up with more integrity and wholeness in your own being leads to greater joy.

Part IV explores the evolution of your identities within community now that you have had time to welcome and accept them. Once you re-shape aspects of yourself, certain aspects and new practices or habits may feel unfamiliar. Practicing with others on a similar path is like building our support scaffold for further growth.

Part I - Unleash

Who Am I? The Search for Identity

Figure 1: Word Cloud of Identities [2] for Cristy

Who Are You?

Who are you? What are the ways you define yourself? Could you fill an entire book (or library) with aspects of your identity if asked? When called upon to introduce yourself, do you feel anxiety over knowing what to select as most relevant?

When I set out to write this book it required me to take time to explore myself and the many layers of my identity more thoroughly. Even after I wrote the first draft, I looked back to see that I was mining my own stories to figure out who I really am, and what I am meant to do in this world.

---

[2] Note: Ambiverts exhibit qualities of both introverts and extroverts. Their preferences are context-dependent rather than fixed.

There are so many layers we encounter when exploring who we are at a deep and fundamental level. For me these started with my parental and familial origins and my cultural identities. They include aspects of my life story which I have told to others to help them understand my perspective in various contexts. They included beliefs and values that I hold dear, and a set of life experiences I have lived. They incorporated the ways that others have defined me in their limited understanding of who I am and painful internalized stereotypes that arose in parallel.

The layers that make up our identity include roles we play, and titles we hold in our jobs. There are activities, preferences, and aversions we develop over time. There are possessions that people hold up as representations of themselves. These may turn out to be temporary markers of phases in our lives, yet they related to parts of our identity, or how we identify ourselves.

Take a moment to consider the parts of your identity.

What is most prominent about you in the outside world?

How do you see yourself from the inside?

Are there parts of your identity you find easy to appreciate?

Are there parts that you wish you could change?

The Outer Layers Versus the Inner Layers

Who we are to the outside world never fully reflects the nuance and complexity of our inner world. Yet others may categorize and define us in ways that dismiss or minimize our fuller identities as unique individuals. What comes to mind immediately is our reflexive labeling of others we encounter around race, gender, and social class. Most of us have minds that prefer certainty and definition. It is comforting to know where we stand in relation to others. However, when this lens is applied in reverse and others make shortcut assumptions about us, it is disconcerting.

While I am interested in the dynamics of how we represent ourselves through our outer layers, that is not where we will focus in this book. I am most interested in those qualities that are selectively hidden when we feel they are out of place, particularly in a work context. We may have been conditioned to hide for very good reasons. I will explore situations that you will likely find familiar and discuss how we navigate what can feel like perilous waters.

Psychologist Carl Rogers believed our self-concept includes three parts: the ideal self (the person we want to be), our self-image (how we see ourselves) and our self-esteem (how much we like and value ourselves). While this may be useful, I prefer a more multi-dimensional notion because social and cultural context matter. We may show up one way in a setting where we are well-known, such as with family or among known work colleagues. On the other hand, we might be liberated of our usual self-concept constraints when we travel to another country or meet people who have no preconceived notions of us.

Ethnicity, Family, and Identity

What about our sense of ethnicity and origin? What is the significance that my father is Mexican and that my mother had parents who were Swedish and English? Are there immigrant stories here that frame the ways I relate to the world? Does the restlessness I often feel harken back to how my ancestors moved to escape difficult economic circumstances in their home countries?

From the outside, you might not realize I am half Mexican. I have dark hair and brown eyes, but my skin is light. My nose and facial features may give me away a bit – the broad nose and dark eyes are gifts from my dad, among other things. The other parts of my appearance and my heritage obscure the certainty to many who meet me without knowing my last name. I often receive a quizzical look when someone cannot quite "place" me ethnically as we are being introduced.

I identify strongly with the "white" and Scandinavian and English part of my heritage also. Great Grandma Alfreda arrived from Sweden in 1880 at age five. My great grandfather, Henry, died of blood poisoning when Alfreda was forty-two, leaving her seven children to raise on her own. The grit and stubbornness it took to manage under those circumstances (while declining proposals of marriage) is something I surely inherited. While some might frame those qualities negatively, others may see them as showing resilience in the face of adversity.

I have unconsciously and consciously "covered" my Mexican heritage, except to those who know my last name. But even when they do know my name, a colleague recently reacted with surprise when I told her I am Latina. She assumed my last name was because of marriage, not birth. Yes, I am THAT white-looking. It also made me realize how I have made a practice of defying stereotypes during my lifetime, so as not to give anyone an excuse to undervalue me. You know the stereotypes about Mexican women, right? We are too emotional (so some claim), and we will keep your house clean (hell no, attests my husband).

What about you? What are the parts of your family, ethnic or cultural heritage where you align most?

Are there aspects of cultural identity you downplay because of stereotypes?

How does it feel to cover an aspect of yourself?

Personality Assessments

I enjoy taking personality tests, strengths finder assessments, and other types of categorical quizzes. In my search for identity, I used to cling to these validated "scientific" definitions to understand myself. However, you will see from the example below that my belief is that personalities can change over time and are dependent on context, circumstances, and personal growth.

The Meyers-Briggs (MBTI) assessment was developed by two non-psychologists who had extensively studied Carl Jung's theory of psychological types[3]. The intention of this tool is to build an understanding of strengths and blind spots and to determine personality preferences along a series of four preference pairs. My Meyers-Briggs type went from INTJ before college, to INFP after college, to ENFP after serving as a manager for a few years. That last test is in doubt for me and initially dismissed it as flawed. I prefer to claim my introvert qualities and require ample solitude to show up at my best. I accept that I may be more of an ambivert depending on context and would never say that "extrovert" describes me.

There have been critiques of the MBTI assessment in recent years and we must use it with a grain of salt. My own example, with only one of the four categories remaining stable in a 25-year span from the first to the most recent, fuels my speculation about our environment's influence on our personality development. While the MBTI can provide broad categories for our preferences, the binary nature of the categories does not reflect the full spectrum of attributes or development across the lifespan.

Understanding aspects of how we prefer to approach and relate to the world can be helpful. I prefer to use a

---

3 https://www.themyersbriggs.com/en-US/Support/MBTI-Facts

CliftonStrengths[4] assessment with my coaching clients. I like the way it gives granularity to a set of our top five or ten strengths from a group of thirty-four distinct categories. It has extensive data sets for statistical validation that I find impressive as a clinical researcher. This tool can offer practical ways to focus on those aspects which are most relevant in the roles and teams where we work or even how we conduct our home life. For those of us who have been advised to improve on our weaknesses, the notion of instead maximizing our strengths feels like a breath of fresh air.

When I hear someone using a tool like the enneagram or their astrological sign to explain who they are, my inner skeptic raises its eyebrows. At this point, I have not yet taken the enneagram. However, I can relate to a feeling of "aha!" that people may experience when an assessment sheds some light on a part of themselves that they have puzzled to understand. To me, the popularity of all these tests and assessments highlights our yearning to know ourselves better.

What about you? How strongly do you identify with the personality tests or other assessments of your strengths?

Have they helped you to know yourself better?

---

4 https://www.gallup.com/cliftonstrengths/en/253676/how-cliftonstrengths-works.aspx

Can you recall times when you contradicted the expectations of these categories?

Is there a difference between tests you have sought out and those that others have required you to take?

The Masks We Wear – Shame and Identities

What about the aspects of our identity or personality which make us uncomfortable? What about troublesome aspects of ourselves which we prefer not to share with others? How can we work with these parts of us?

Social scientist and researcher Brené Brown speaks and writes eloquently about the corrosive effects of shame on our lives[5]. She makes distinctions between shame and guilt that I will explore here because they helped me understand my impulse to hide parts of myself. Dr. Brown explains that shame is a focus on self and guilt is a focus on behavior. If we do something that does not live up to our values, feeling guilt might sound like, "I should not have done that, it was a mistake," and we may feel regret. If we feel shame, the response might be: "Why did I do that? **I am bad.**"

The difference may seem subtle, but it is critically important when it comes to accepting ourselves despite our perceived flaws and imperfections. When we hurt someone or do something we do not feel proud of, guilt allows us to admit the mistake and perhaps to make amends. Of course, unresolved guilt carries weight, and it is worth conscious self-inquiry if we become aware it is affecting us. If we feel shame for the behavior and attribute it to something that is inherently wrong with us, the resulting action will be to hide rather than to take ownership and try to behave differently in the future.

Shame over who we are tends to shut out further learning and growth. High levels of shame correlate with addiction, eating disorders, depression, and other mental health struggles. Shame makes us feel as though we are not worthy of love and belonging. We may feel that something is inherently wrong with

---

[5] Summarized from *The Gifts of Imperfection* (2010) and *The Power of Vulnerability: Teachings on Authenticity, Connection & Courage* audio speeches (2013).

us rather than accepting that all humans are flawed, and that everyone makes mistakes. All humans are worthy of love and belonging even when we may not show up at our best all the time.

Back when I was in elementary school, I had trouble keeping my desk neat. In those days we didn't get traditional letter grades. There was "E" for "excellent," "S" for "satisfactory," and "N" for "needs improvement." My academics were always E or S, but when it came to "keeps belongings neat and tidy" on the report card, this was **one BIG N** in my mind. My mom used to refer to me affectionately as "pig pen" because I always seemed to have something sticky on me, and I couldn't keep my room organized to save my life. When Dad struggled to find things or was forgetful, we called him an "absentminded professor." I would have preferred a professor identity to the image of Charlie Brown's little dust-generating sidekick. I am still curious about how the same exact traits in men and women are seen differently and characterized in positive or negative ways through gendered lenses.

Later I will explain how learning about my attention deficit disorder (ADHD/ADD) just before I turned thirty helped me understand why certain types of activities like organization are more challenging. Rather than take it on as an identity (a messy person) or a character flaw, I have reframed it as an area where I consciously request support without making it mean anything negative about me.

Is there anything about yourself or your identity that you experience as shameful?

If so, where do you feel this emotion in your body?

How about any areas where you feel guilty about your behavior?

Can you allow yourself forgiveness for your past mistakes?

Did anyone give you a pet name you found annoying? How did this affect your image of yourself?

Losing and Reclaiming the Smart Girl Identity

I recall the Dean's bearded face and twinkling Santa Claus eyes looking at me from across the lovely mahogany desk that was guarding him. After my story and my tearful confession of worries he said, "It's not as though you've been struck stupid!"

But he was wrong. That's EXACTLY what it felt like. I was a senior in college, a second year Resident Assistant (RA) for my dorm, considered one of the smart ones, the "together" ones. I was a biochemistry major and pre-med at the time. And yet: when I tried to count the bacterial colonies for my independent study with a professor, my head swam with confusion. I kept mixing up the protocols and I couldn't seem to figure out why. My lab notebook was a mess, and I couldn't seem to follow the instructions.

Physical chemistry class was like trying to make out an ancient obscure language without a translation dictionary or the faintest idea of grammar. Even the subjects I loved felt like a slog to complete the reading, while before I had lapped them up like a cat with milk. What was happening in my brain?!? Did I somehow manage to fake my smarts enough to get through three years at Swarthmore and now my fraudulent "lazy girl" hidden identity was letting herself out of the bag? Had I hit my head without knowing it?

Fortunately, I did not let the Dean's denial of my visceral experience get to me. I persisted in trying to find a trusted advisor to get help. When a friend suggested, "Why don't you try Psych Services at the Health Center?" I quivered. Oh dear. I'm an RA! What will my hallmates think if their trusted advisor can't figure her sh*t out on her own? Nevertheless, I knew I needed help. The cognitive fog in my brain was not normal, and other physical symptoms like intense sugar cravings and sleep disturbances were not helping. I swallowed my pride and scheduled an appointment.

In only a few sessions with my kind therapist, I started feeling such relief. I discovered how negative my self-talk was, and how viciously I had attacked myself for not being able to achieve what I knew I could do (normally). I had not even been aware of the litany of attacks that had become my constant internal monologue. I did not know this self-loathing would have such a detrimental effect on my body and mind.

Through cognitive behavior therapy (CBT) and a return to my journaling practice, I was able to identify thoughts that were not serving me. I started to question and "loosen" some of those beliefs that were causing me so much pain. Within a couple months, I visited with my adviser to consider a change in my major. The move to psychobiology served my passion for understanding behavior and people, and I had taken all the prerequisites. I ended up graduating on time with high marks on my "comps," the final essays required for the special major.

My self-talk had been negative and berating. I had been telling myself a story of weakness and laziness. All those voices from elementary and middle school, from teachers who told my parents I was smart but not working up to my potential, rose to confirm that was true. Even though I saw myself as smart, these internalized oppressive voices told me I was lazy. If only I would try harder, I would be able to transcend this issue.

I had not realized how much the identity of the "lazy smart girl" had come to define me and the way I saw myself. When I saw that identity crumbling before my eyes during an episode of clinical depression, I was forced to ask: what else about my identity is important? What if it is not just my smarts that define me? What if I can choose to define myself in other ways?

All the while during that year my old self-identification ("smart but lazy") was undergoing tremendous change. Depression can feel like a dark and endless cave, or like a thick, soupy brain fog that makes all decisions difficult. Recovery can feel like emerging from a cocoon to fly, after a huge effort to work off what is confining us. My identity had shifted profoundly. I realized I was a still a "smart woman" and so much more than that. I was not lazy, and I had been doing my best. I no longer feared that, if something happened to my smarts, I would be nobody. My self-concept began to incorporate my kindness and my deep empathy for others along with being smart.

I share this story so that you can understand how our identities can be shaped by internal narratives and beliefs we may not even realize. Circumstances may arise that destroy a false identity or negative self-belief we have used as a shield. This prompts us to peel back the layers of our assumptions to question what is true. Then we may need to heal those parts of our psyche that clung to the old lies or painful beliefs we mistakenly adopted. It wasn't until my late twenties when another episode of depression eventually led to a correct diagnosis of attention deficit hyperactivity disorder (ADHD). This helped me prevent the cyclical trend toward overwork and burnout that tipped me toward depression and anxiety. I will address this later in the book in the section on diagnoses and identity.

What is important here is that our bodies respond to the stories (and lies) we tell ourselves, especially those that are on repetitive loops. If we mercilessly beat ourselves up over who we are or something we did, this takes not just a psychological toll, but a physical and biochemical one. Unlearning those unkind lies with the help of a counselor, mentor, or coach can be a key to our liberation.

Take heart if whatever transition you are in feels difficult now. This is liminal space, and you are going to emerge stronger. Your inherent magnificence is not dependent on anything you do, or who you are in a narrow sense. As you come to know yourself in a more complete way and embrace parts of you that you may have hidden before, you may surprise yourself with discoveries. It is brave work, and it can be profoundly rewarding when you are ready.

Do you feel like you've ever lost a part of your identity or that something about you was called into question?

How did you cope?

Were there activities, resources, or people who helped you gain perspective?

The Error of Equating Behaviors to Identity

Bringing this back to the distinctions between shame and guilt, please be careful not to attribute your behaviors solely to some aspect of your identity. Sometimes behaviors arise from early learning before we were conscious enough to understand why we were adopting these patterns. I sometimes hear clients or friends saying something like, "that's just the way I am," as though there is something unchangeable about our tendencies. We all learn, grow, and develop new skills throughout our lifespan. It is true that many of us are challenged by different wiring, but in my experience, all humans are as capable of growth as they are of breathing.

When I first learned that my wiring is consistent with ADHD, I was completely puzzled. I am not hyperactive, but my attention is variable. This is one of the key reasons why until later in life, women and girls are typically under-diagnosed. There are three "presentations" in this type of phenomenon: hyperactive, inattentive, or combination types. For me, I was able to quell my restlessness by escaping into my imagination. Thus I didn't present a behavior problem for teachers in the classroom.

Girls and women with ADHD often mask our symptoms by becoming perfectionists and obsessively checking our work. Compulsive behaviors around eating, working hard, and people-pleasing can become compensating behaviors for the anxiety that results from not trusting ourselves.

Are there any behaviors or habits you feel are central to your identity?

When did these behaviors begin?

Diagnoses Do Not Define Our Identities

If you have received any mental health diagnoses, like depression, anxiety, or other "temperament" disorders, please know that these do not define you. Jenara Nerenberg makes a convincing case in her book, *Divergent Mind,* that historically, women have been pathologized for sensitivity and "hysteria" with no consideration for their inner life. Ironically, Nerenberg says, "women are systematically left out of research studies in favor of obtaining streamlined, publishable results that otherwise risk being tainted by the presence of women and their hormones.[6]" As a clinical researcher, I am appalled at the absurdity that we can generalize from studies of men alone.

The most important thing about receiving a diagnosis is that it can greatly impact effective treatments for areas where we may suffer. During my second episode of depression, I greatly benefitted from medication and therapy. That time the darkness had arisen in the summer for me, unusual in that it had been my favorite season before, and I love the extra light. Therapy was not enough to pull me from the depths, and I was grateful that selective serotonin uptake inhibitors (SSRIs) were there to provide the additional support while my brain chemistry was coming back into balance.

When I was first diagnosed with ADHD, it came at the tail end of a nearly year-long depression cycle. My nurse practitioner noticed that I'd received a surge of energy when I became involved in a political campaign. Then I went into another crash. Could this be cyclothymia, a less severe form of bipolar disorder? The medicine she prescribed was not helping. I kept wondering if I "wasn't trying hard enough." During one appointment she thought to ask if I had ever been evaluated for ADHD. I scoffed! I was in graduate school, working on my

---

[6] *Divergent Mind* p. 42

master's thesis. Surely someone who had made it through college couldn't have ADHD, could they? Also, I hated the sound of having a "deficit disorder." I didn't experience myself as someone with a deficit. Now I understand how many in the ADHD community define our behavioral traits as differences, not disorders.

Typically, the symptoms of ADHD as they present in childhood include impulsivity, distractibility, restlessness, poor working memory, difficulty staying organized, and time blindness. However, since the stereotype of a restless boy disrupting a classroom still receives the most attention, a girl with inattentive ADHD may experience internal restlessness and boredom. Though it may not look obvious, if she is not challenged, she may "check-out" during classes. Or if her mother sends her to clean her room, she may find a book she had been looking for and start reading. Hours later, when Mom checks on her, she has completely forgotten about the request to clean. A mundane and boring task gets dropped while the more interesting forgotten book takes center stage.

Once the evaluation was complete and I started receiving proper medical treatment with a stimulant medication, I could finally function without the constant scatterbrained and frantic feeling that I was forgetting something. Within two years, the master's thesis that I kept procrastinating finally got completed. The absentminded professor part of me suddenly realized she COULD get things done if she learned to structure her time and projects appropriately. It was also necessary to exercise my body much more regularly and to keep my neurochemistry healthy. Knowing I was not neurotypical meant I needed different kinds of support to keep my brain healthy. This helped me discover running, along with an amazing community of support for this endeavor. It also helped me become a successful operations manager for an international team at a medical device company.

The set of traits mentioned above is a subset of the diagnostic criteria. It is now being redefined by Dr. Edward Hallowell, (an authority on ADHD) as **VAST: variable attention stimulus trait**. I love this reframing of a condition that is not always a deficit and can be an asset in certain lines of work. VAST is more neutral and more accurate. Clearly someone with a neurotypical way of being came up with ADHD. They were using it to describe an externally observed set of characteristics. Earlier in human history, before the industrial era required "productivity and "efficiency" models that reward conformity and uniformity, our traits were seen as gifts. Our unique ways of seeing new possibilities and being more sensitive to certain stimuli might be valued as leadership qualities in some circumstances. The inability to conform to a linear model of learning, or the need for more kinesthetic or active processing might serve to help others question the status quo. In a world where so many systems need reform, our inability to simply go along with the crowd might be an advantage, not a deficit.

When I first began exploring my diagnosis with ADHD, I had to process the grief and pain that come from realizing I had innocently believed those teachers who had said I was "not working up to my potential" year after year. I mourned the loss of years which I spent criticizing myself for these traits, wishing I could be more like other people, and hiding these aspects as best I could. I feel tremendous self-compassion for this closeted part of my identity. And now I feel particularly committed to advocating for those who think and process in different ways, creating communities and workplaces where we can embrace our gifts in ways others can receive them.

In case you are tempted to identify with a diagnosis and say something like "I am anxious," see how it feels to say, "I am feeling anxious right now," instead. Or try describing what you feel in your body, like tightness in the chest or shoulders, or heat in the solar plexus. While it is a subtle change in framing, it can help you to take a step back from identifying with a specific diagnosis and to note the qualities that are happening in your body. You might see how the qualities fluctuate and oscillate rather than experiencing them as a constant.

Do you have any formal or informal "diagnoses" that frame your identity?

Can you accept these as only one facet of yourself?

Can you experience the multitudes contained within you beyond these medicalized terms?

Identity and Career Status

Many people in Western cultures strongly identify what we "do" for money and career as inherent to our identities. This is a slippery slope if we undergo a major career change or a layoff while we identified too strongly with a particular identity that's tied to our career. Also, many of us work "day jobs" that fund the creative aspirations that may not yet (or ever) cover all our bills. Are we still an author if we currently work as a receptionist and our book income is not yet paying us what we need to live? Absolutely. In fact, I would argue that it might be necessary for us to make a sacred commitment to these inner identities, even when the world is not kind to our aspirations. Fearful people who may have abandoned their dreams may feel the need to "warn" you that your dreams are too big. This is not about you or your potential, this is about them. Keep going, especially if something in your spirit keeps beckoning you forward.

For many years I called myself a clinical researcher. It was an identity that I was proud to explain to others on airplanes or when introduced. Many of my mentors wanted to see more women and girls in the sciences, especially Latinas, and my ego enjoyed the feeling of prestige this career label afforded me. When I went from this career to returning to my "roots" as a teacher, facilitator, coach, it was disconcerting at first. Others knew me (and many still know me) as a clinical researcher and have respect for this profession.

Aspects of my Medtronic identity and affiliation were coveted and admired. As an operations manager and geography leader in an organization that was highly competitive, this status earned respect from my colleagues. Even my husband, who was initially supportive of my recent change in direction, has asked me if I could return to a role that was more like the one that provided us generous frequent flyer miles to support our travel adventures. But my body gives me a firm and clear "no" on this notion, so I continue to follow this embodied wisdom. Our careers are often a status marker, not necessarily a mirror for our deeper identity.

How have your career choices related to your identity?

Have you made any large career pivots that required rethinking your identity?

Identity, Purpose, and Future Self

Our identity often becomes linked to our purpose. For those that identify as nurses or doctors, for example, this purpose might be to heal people, to alleviate suffering, or to aid those in need. But for those of us who are wired to have many different careers in our lifetime, this sense of purpose may look differently than a linear path. There may be an important and necessary set of skills we are learning for future opportunities. We may not even know when we initially take a job that there is an overarching purpose. It is not always possible to anticipate how that will play out, except in retrospect as we reflect and inhabit the lessons we have learned in our lives.

I recently had a networking interview with someone who was trying to understand my transition from nonprofit and educational work to a position in clinical research for the device industry. She wanted to know more. The truth of the matter is that the economy prior to the housing crisis meltdown in 2008 was not great for nonprofits. I was offered a contract at twice the pay of positions in the nonprofit world and wanted money to rebuild my foundation after my divorce. It was less about a lofty sense of purpose than it was about finding an opportunity where I knew I would keep learning new things while being paid generously. I am not ashamed to admit that. We meet many different needs through our work, and our ultimate purpose may or may not be linked.

Future Self as a Guide

It can be motivating to adopt the characteristics of identities or future selves which we aspire to reach. I like to imagine myself as a successful published author and public speaker. This is an aspiration for my future self, and my daily actions can keep moving me in that direction. When I ask myself, "What would a successful published author do?" when it comes to editing, it occurs to me that working with a professional editor is an important part of my journey. Thus, finding an editor came from visualizing an identity that I imagine as part of my future self. The more actions I take to embody the author identity, the more possibilities and wisdom emerge for me to take the next right step without necessarily knowing the entire path.

Does your sense of identity relate to your purpose in life?

Has your sense of purpose ever wavered in the face of internal or external changes?

How did this impact your identity?

Severing Ourselves from Marginalized Identities

For those of us with marginalized identities, many of us have been persuaded or nudged to divide and sever ourselves from the wisdom of our somatic (embodied) experiences. We have learned to rely on our minds and our intellect as though our bodies are a "lesser" part of ourselves. Often religious indoctrination plays a part in this, with biblical descriptions characterizing the "base" and bodily desires of humans as below spiritual concerns. And while most of us can relate to some conflicting desires within us, divorcing our bodily needs and desires from our inherent wholeness is a trap. We need to redevelop our connection to all parts of our inner experience rather than shut down those that the mainstream culture deems inconvenient.

Maybe you are a person of mixed ethnic heritage who has been told "you don't look Mexican" (like me) because of your light skin color. Or someone was surprised that you were Mexican because, "you're so articulate." While these microaggressions may have seemed innocuous and innocent to the person who intended this as a compliment, they reinforced painful stereotypes by prompting us to question our belonging. We might have felt relief about not being lumped into the group of "those other Mexicans." We may also feel some shame at not knowing how to resolve the otherness that has now been cast on us, while effectively standing up for the Mexicans that have been denigrated by this casual remark.

Passing or covering as white is something bicultural people do to assimilate into work cultures, and it is not without a cost. It can cause us to sink and shrink inward, physically, and emotionally, a form of somatic colonization. Where is it safe to really be our full selves? What does it mean to be Mexican? What does it mean to have a hidden psychological disability when we already feel othered? How are others using aspects of our identities to define us, when we know that we are more than those stereotypical caricatures?

I did not understand until recently how these subtle and not-so-subtle barbs enacted real and lasting effects in my body. I did not realize my own somatic "contractions" are responses to the ways in which people have othered me until I started practicing soma yoga. I was finally able to release those old shapes and memories held in my body. It started to connect for me conceptually when I first read Resmaa Menakem's book, *My Grandmother's Hands.*

Menakem articulates eloquently the ways in which racism and racial trauma imprint themselves within our bodies and nervous systems. Legacies of intergenerational trauma are passed down to families and communities when they are not healed. This is not just a mental process, but an all-encompassing physical and somatic one. Studies of epigenetics are now revealing to us the extent to which generational experiences become encoded into genetic expression. To heal these wounds requires embodied and somatic practices for releasing that go beyond merely a "talk therapy" model. While therapy may be an important first step in healing, my personal journey has shown that it was not sufficient to change long-ingrained habits and patterns that are somatically held.

As I share this notion of severing our internal parts, take a few moments to breathe and scan your body.

Do you have memories of contraction or shrinking? Are there people, places, or events that come to mind?

What about memories of expansion? Are there people, places or events that come to mind?

Can you imagine a feeling of unity with all the parts of yourself?

What would it take to feel this? Don't intellectualize this question; just answer from your intuitive notions, even if the answers seem strange or vague.

Identities in the Workplace

I hope that you have at least a couple of trusted people in your life, and maybe at your workplace, with whom you share deeper aspects of who you are without shame. If you do not have these trusted people right now, I encourage you to seek friends, a coach, mentor, therapist, or counselor who can provide nonjudgmental and caring support to you. There is no shame in seeking help. I have reached out multiple times in my life, especially when I knew big changes were brewing within me. This includes the time while writing this book. Peeling back layers of protection may feel vulnerable and sensitive, and receiving witness from a trained facilitator is one way to assist our healing.

You may need to seek support especially during transitions such as a change in marital status, a career or job shift, or other stressful life events. While you navigate these changes, it may impact your ability to show up fully at work or home. Please be gentle with yourself during these liminal times. For those who lead or manage employees, be aware that major identity shifts, which are part of human development, may require effort and energy on the part of the people you lead. If your organization provides Employee Assistance Program (EAP) services, let your employees know they can access resources in that way for confidential support. There are some of us who find it harder to ask for help due to family or cultural conditioning. When a kind boss who notices our distress can steer us in the direction of good self-care rather than shaming us for not performing as we normally might, this inspires greater trust and loyalty.

We live in a world where change continues to accelerate. We all want to use our gifts in ways that can maximize our impact. To this end, it becomes important to explore your identities and to come to terms with any "orphaned" parts of yourself. We often carry stories that drive choices that are not nourishing to us or beneficial in the long term. (For me, this can mean reaching for sugar when I'm feeling sad or scared.) These become habits, and we need to give ourselves compassion for some part of us that was attempting to care for itself. And then when we realize that these old habits may be leading in an unhealthy direction, we can become conscious and choose differently. Many of us, especially women, were socialized to put our needs last. Long-term, this has devastating effects on our health and the vitality of our planet.

Since most of us spend almost a third of our waking hours at work, it is important to find workplaces where we can show up with integrity and a sense of being okay just as we are. This does not mean we do not strive for improvement and growth. But any workplace where we do not feel it is okay to be ourselves will claim more energy to contribute than a place where our gifts are valued and encouraged. Our search may not be easy. It took me until my mid-thirties to find a place where I was able to be myself on a more regular basis. I stayed there for eleven years and received three promotions. Take heart. You will find your people (though not always at work) and you will continue to learn more about your interests, gifts, and desires along the way.

Cultivating friendships outside of work can help also. Work is important, but it is not all that your life is about. If your friends come only from your workplace, it could feel traumatic to get downsized or have a work catastrophe that separates you from valuable support systems. I realize my perspective reflects some privilege. I have had parents and friends that were incredibly supportive during periods of career transition in my life. It is always worth cultivating friends (I call them my "chosen family") who love you as you are and not for what you do for them.

Do you have friends or colleagues who support you at work?

Do you have friends or colleagues outside of work who support you?

If you cannot think of anyone at this moment, what is one step you can take to move toward building a tiny (but mighty) team to support you?

When will you commit to taking this step? Commit to an actual date and write it down.

Troublesome Hidden Identities

You are a beautiful soul. You can love everything about you. However, it can be difficult (or even impossible) to "let it all hang out" at work. There is a part of you that you may feel the need to withhold from more mainstream colleagues. Kenji Yoshino, a Chief Justice Earl Warren Professor of Constitutional Law at NYU School of Law, refers to this practice as "covering."[7] This is different from passing in that it may involve muting or downplaying differences rather than hiding them completely.

President Franklin Delano Roosevelt always hosted press briefings or had photographs taken from behind a desk. While the reporters knew he used a wheelchair he minimized the relevance of his disability. He kept the focus on traits that were seen as more "Presidential"—he was a distinguished white man, and these qualities were front and center. Imagine how much further the disability rights movement might have progressed had he shown an example of a wartime President who was able to function from his wheelchair during a critical period in history.

Workplaces may not ever embrace our whole selves. Thus it is important to learn to listen to our intuition when it comes to knowing how much to share. While I never advocate for people to be inauthentic at work, we must sense our psychological safety before completely opening up. The micro-practices in Part III of this book will help you develop greater intuition to discern when covering is oppressive versus when it is adaptive. This is something that can be taken in stages and as you get to know people; it is not a one-time event. Trust is earned over time, and we have no obligation to grant it before that time.

---

[7] https://www.linkedin.com/learning/uncovering-your-authentic-self-at-work/covering-and-your-work

Is there any part of you that you feel compelled to hide from your boss or your peers?

What is your greatest fear about revealing yourself?

Can you have compassion for any misunderstanding others may have about your hidden qualities?

Also, is it truly possible to keep them hidden?

Where might they spill out despite your efforts to hide them?

Leadership and Stereotypes

When I began leadership training as part of a high potential cohort of Latine managers and directors at Medtronic, we were assigned to write and tell our "leadership story." This felt like an important effort, to understand the aspects of myself that had brought me to the current situation where I was being called to lead in a large and complex company.

I struggled to decide what I wanted to share: Do I tell people I had to go against so many of the things I was taught to arrive at this spot? Do I share my experiences with depression? Do I talk about getting married in my early twenties and divorced by the time I was thirty? Can I be open about the fact that others have seen me as a leader many times in my life when I had no interest in leading? Can I explain how being a bicultural person feels like "odd person out" much of the time, but that I have learned to see it as an asset for me to understand multiple perspectives?

Many of my colleagues focused on more traditional facets of their journeys. Training for certain careers, a decade of focused work, etc. As a highly intuitive person, I like to sense the energy in the room before deciding what level of safety is present. This can mean that I have more than one version of a speech prepared when it comes to this kind of assignment. While some might see this adaptation as guarded or less authentic, I like the way Adam Grant refers to this as high self-monitoring and adaptive to the situation[8].

Let's face it: **stereotypes exist and persist around our marginalized identities.** This is usually why we downplay them. My set of fears around outing my neurodiversity relate to stereotypes about being disorganized, flaky, and unreliable. And from the opening story, you might gather that I am not

---

8 https://www.ted.com/talks/worklife_with_adam_grant_your_hidden_personality

great at taking direction from leadership if I believe they are on the wrong path. I am extremely dedicated and hyper-focused on efforts and projects I find compelling. I can be like a dog with a bone when it comes to advocating for something that is meaningful to me.

When I am on a mission, I am driven. It can be a detriment to my wellness that I "lose track" of my body and somatic awareness if I do not take conscious breaks to check in. I also influence others easily when I believe in something deeply. People might see this as irrational exuberance, especially if they cannot see how I arrived at a conclusion with which they disagree.

Taking ownership of my ADHD qualities, which are typically described as "executive function" challenges, meant understanding how and why ADHD and leadership often go together. While estimates vary, some studies report that 30-50 percent of entrepreneurs have ADHD brains[9]. This seems like a paradox at first. But this mystery is resolved when we operate with a team and begin to focus on our areas of strength while hiring or collaborating with others who have different strengths. While we can be impulsive and may take more risks than a neurotypical person, we also tend to solve problems in novel ways. As we learn to work with our tendencies, we develop more maturity in our approach. We can also build systems to help us take calculated risks that contain safety margins.

Do you have a leadership story?

---

[9] "Creative Energy Optimized (C.E.O.)," *ADDitude Magazine*, Winter 2021

Are there times in your life when you have led people at work or in a less conventional way?

If you see yourself as a leader, what experiences contributed to this identity?

If not, what holds you back from seeing yourself as a leader?

Even if you do not lead in the traditional sense, are there times when others looked to you for guidance?

Enlisting Help and Support

I now see my enthusiasm and energy as a beautiful quality. I also know that I may need to enlist others in helping me communicate passions in ways that are more logical or methodical for others who are not able to make the same conceptual leaps. Having what Dr. Hallowell calls a "Ferrari brain with bicycle brakes,"[10] means I need to design into my schedule time for transitions. I also ask loved ones to help me stay accountable to take breaks, and step away from my work periodically. This way I don't stay stuck in any "mental wind tunnels" that pull me along without being mindful that my direction is still aligned. If you do not have someone sharing your space that can help you do this, you might consider planning time with a friend or colleague in advance.

You may have learned to feel shame over asking for help, or if you do have a neurodiverse brain, you may struggle with rejection sensitive dysphoria[11]. This is a more extreme emotional sensitivity and perception of rejection and criticism from people in our lives. I don't love how many phrases invoke a sense of pathology related to ADHD (and here's another one). But the reason I mention this concept is that once I understood it, I was less hard on myself about knowing why asking is so difficult for me. Neurotypical people don't seem to internalize rejection the way we might, and knowing this, we can prepare ourselves in a different way. In writing this manuscript, I've worked with this tendency, realizing that how others receive my work is beyond my control. And if someone doesn't want to read my work, it's not because they don't like me. It could be that the topic just doesn't resonate with them.

---

[10] https://drhallowell.com/2019/04/05/your-adhd-brain-is-a-ferrari/
[11] https://www.additudemag.com/rejection-sensitive-dysphoria-adhd-symptom-test/

If you are new at your workplace and you don't know people well yet, you can search online accountability groups that can help. In the ADHD world we call this practice "body doubling," when we work alongside someone else, either in person or virtually. There are coworking groups that feel like an "adult study hall." I recently found a person in my network that meets with me monthly to work on tasks like organizing paperwork (a task where we both tend to procrastinate). We meet via Zoom for 90 minutes and typically chat for the first 10 minutes and the last 5 minutes to check in. It is harder to wiggle out of something when a kind face is on the other end of the call, and I will have to report how the session went.

Now that so many more people are working in remote places and outside of offices, the number of virtual coworking opportunities has proliferated. Several of my favorite ADHD podcasters recommend "Focus mate." I have not tried that one yet, but some people swear by it. It can take some time to find the right fit here, so if it doesn't work the first time, you may need to shop around for a better fit. Most programs have a low-cost or free introductory period so you can try before committing resources.

How often do you ask for help?

Do you feel comfortable with asking others for support?

Do you ever feel like asking for help is cheating?

Do you fear rejection when you ask for help?

What are ways you can ask for help in a way that makes room emotionally for any response you receive, without taking it personally?

Complementary Strengths

Our unique sets of strengths can be leveraged in greater ways when coupled with the right complementary strengths of others. For example, my top strength as characterized by the CliftonStrengths tool is as a "Relator." I find it easy to connect with people. I do this intuitively and typically form close relationships easily. However, there are people with a "Focus" strength that are much better at executing the follow through on a project because they excel at prioritization and action.

Somewhere in my top ten is "Arranger" so I have the flexibility to organize and re-group when necessary. However, I enjoy working with people who have an "Activator" strength that are eager to turn thoughts into action. "Intellection" is number three on my list, meaning that I love to think. The trap is when I overuse that strength and overthink rather than taking action to move forward. Finding people on our teams with complementary strengths and explicitly talking together about how we tend to use them has been transformative for me in the way I approach projects.

We must develop humility around understanding other qualities that might be perceived as weaknesses. I used to be quite defensive when things like this were pointed out to me. I would stew about these things for days. Now I understand when trust is built with others who are invested in our collective growth, feedback is easier to receive. I can ask for accountability on the improvements I wish to embody. If you are new to a team or have not yet found your ideal work situation, realize that others' feedback is as much about their preferences as it is about any shortcomings on your part. It is also possible that we might find ourselves in roles that do not make the best use of our gifts. If we stay open to the feedback, it may help nudge us either to improve or move toward a different job or function that is a better fit.

What are YOUR strengths?

Have you had someone tell you that you're good at something?

Even if you don't use the CliftonStrengths terms like I did, how would you describe a couple of activities where you excel?

Do you have opportunities to use your strengths every day, or at least a few times a week?

Support for Our Evolving Identities

I currently employ a coach and other project partners to help me periodically. I have also enlisted the support of my husband, friends, and colleagues. I still have the impulse to hide my perceived failings rather than to be open about where I want or need support. Like many things, this gets easier the more we practice. When we do not ask for what we want, how will others know how to support us? A good friend and financial advisor had pens printed with "You don't get 100% of what you don't ask for." (Thank you, Josue Castillo.) Can you absorb the profound truth of this statement? Also, don't assume that you need to pay for this support necessarily. Sometimes we can arrange to barter time with others who have different strengths.

When we take any part of ourselves and shove it away out of shame, we miss what is most unique and delightful about us. Do we find some of own our traits and habits to be annoying sometimes? Of course. I don't enjoy the fact that I tend to misplace things like my phone or my keys. But we can develop reminders and systems for keeping track of important things. I sometimes slip into my "absentminded professor" mode, and then I forget and set things down while I am not fully present. Rather than being annoyed with ourselves when we do these things, can we learn to laugh at ourselves kindly and love our imperfections?

Who supports your growth and evolution?

If you don't have anyone who plays this role right now, can you spend 5 minutes brainstorming possible mentors or "friend-tors[12]"?

The Deepest Part of Our Identity

It is a deep and spiritual question to ask, "Who am I?" It is an object of contemplation for mystics and seekers who want a deeper relationship with themselves and the divine. We want to know who we are beyond the labels and conditioned tendencies. Is there some fundamental and immutable part of us that we access when we observe our innermost being?

Most spiritual traditions claim we have a soul or spirit, that fundamental part of us that never changes, and in some beliefs, never dies. Secular philosophers might call that awareness itself, the part of us that is not weighed down by our various identities. Martha Beck calls this the "watcher." When we become aware of this larger awareness within us, we are lifted out of the temporary fluctuations of the mind. There is larger Self, which I capitalize to distinguish it from the smaller self we define with labels.

When we consider the fundamental need that humans have for belonging and connection, the search for identity makes sense. We want to know not only, "Who am I?" but we want to know, "Where do I belong?" And we also want to know what we are here to do, our purpose for being here. That deep sense of purpose gives us reasons why we get out of bed each day. For most of us, without a sense of purpose and belonging we feel lost and directionless. Knowing who we are and what we stand for is a powerful brew.

For some of us there may not be just "one big thing" that defines our purpose. I prefer to think about purpose in terms of phases in our lives and usually coach people to follow their curiosity instead of their passion. Many of us are multi-passionate. We cannot always articulate in a neat and tidy sentence the one thing we are here to do. If you relate to this, you might enjoy Emilie Wapnick's Ted Talk on "Why Some of Us Don't Have One True Calling."

Can you sense a larger awareness or presence within you that goes beyond all ways that words and ideas limit us?

What gets in the way of feeling this presence?

If this presence I ask about seems elusive to you now, no worries. Some of us are a bit more anxious and have a harder time accessing the wisdom encoded into our bodies. When we get to Part III you will learn a few ways to help stop your over-thinking mind so you can sink into a larger sense of your wisest Self.

Unleash – Why This Term?

While I prefer to avoid terms that are trite or cliché, I chose the word "unleash" not because I am a Tony Robbins fan (quite the contrary). When I think about my own struggle with ADHD, what comes to mind is the image of an eager puppy. My exuberant mind loves moving and bouncing, and it is often full of boundless energy (when it is not exhausted from too much input or administrative details). While we may delight in a small puppy jumping up to lick us on the face, there are times when we are working or on a conference call when the puppy may need a little restraint. We don't need to punish or cage the puppy. A light leash is a gentle reminder that there are times for jumping and licking, and there are times for calmly listening to others without interrupting.

When the puppy's need for love and appreciation gets unbearable, we take off that leash and allow her to express and roam freely. The metaphor works well for me, although untethering or unshackling these aspects of our inner being may feel more relevant to you. Whatever makes your body and soul feel most free is what I hope you use.

Part II- Unlearn

Why Unlearning?

Throughout our lives we are asked to learn many things in school and at work. So why is unlearning more important than learning?

Many of us learned ineffective patterns starting at a young age by adults who were part of a social system that ignored the detrimental effects of suppressing our embodied wisdom. The industrial era required compliant and conforming factory workers to support a capitalist infrastructure. Creative impulses and a more dynamic interplay of movement were not part of many growing classrooms which focused on book-based learning rather than broader ways of knowing. Growing up in a family of teachers, I observed how restrictive some of the requirements could be. Some teachers were able to work around these efforts to standardize curricula, since they intuitively knew that we cannot, nor should we, standardize human beings.

Environmental and economic changes are accelerating faster than in previous generations. Our ability to grow deeper into our consciousness and self-awareness will be the key to humans thriving on this warming planet. We need to experience ourselves as microcosms of our larger world. We need to know, accept, and embrace all parts of ourselves to evolve into who we are meant to become. Learning the interplay of the fractal nature of our relationship in communities and the larger world may help us see how what we do every day has an impact. And we must forgive ourselves and others for past mistakes while making amends when we can.

The problem is that most of us try to do this by using only our minds, not the entire conscious, sensing, moving, and relating BEING in our wholeness. Humans learn behavior patterns as we are socialized in families and communities where many of us gained acceptance by following group norms. The developmental and biochemical nature of our brain is to observe survival patterns of those around us and to imitate similar patterns and habits. It is highly adaptive to pay attention to what garners love and support from our caregivers while we are infants and children to be sure we receive care.

In adolescence, as we begin to differentiate our own identity, it is not uncommon for rebellious behaviors to occur unless we face consequences. As adults, we often start to recognize habits we learned may no longer serve us. Perhaps they never served us, but as children we internalized them in an innocent attempt to keep the peace. We mature and realize the circumstances we are in today are not the same as the ones we navigated while we developed conditioned responses and tendencies. I have observed that conscious daily and weekly practices and habits I develop intentionally have more impact on me than academic knowledge about wellbeing.

Somatics and Embodied Wisdom

If you are going to show up in the world as your brave and authentic self, you will need to fuel your journey. You need to have great fortitude to explore the depths of your being, to learn more about who you are, the light and the shadow and everything in between. Whether you bring all your parts to bear in your outward life, any orphaned stories or abandoned identities may rise in strange ways. And unless you own your stories, they will end up owning you.

As you embark upon this exploration, you will need tools and practices to keep you healthy, balanced, and strong. What I am learning about neuroscience is that our brains are such a small portion of the overall wisdom of our body. Our entire nervous system is involved in activating our behavior, not merely the grey matter in our heads. What if we thought of our full consciousness, which is so much larger than our brain, as distributed throughout the entire soma? Our nervous system is this extension of our consciousness as an integrated, whole, and connected magnificent being.

It is necessary here to define how I am using the word "soma" and "somatic" generally to distinguish this from how this differs from using "body" to when I refer to the practices. Thomas Hanna's seminal work *Somatics* describes the externalized, third-person view as describing a body[13]. In contrast, *soma* comes from a Greek word that means "living body." The living, self-sensing, self-aware, and self-moving perception of oneself from the inside out helps us to see bodies in a multi-dimensional and energetic way. Rather than a collection of parts, the way a pathologist (or even some physicians) might encounter, the somatic viewpoint brings back a sense of agency and self-responsibility. We can change ourselves and shape our futures with our desires, our emotions, and with our actions.

Neuroscience teaches that our frontal cortex is used for executive function and decision making. And some scientists are finding that our gut bacteria and microbiome can drive even more of our behavior than what is "directed" by our heads. Teachers from Eastern disciplines like yoga explain that the solar plexus chakra fuels action, and this seems like no coincidence, though Western science may have been slower to discover it. By nourishing these areas of the body well, we increase the probability that we will be able to act on our intentions. When it comes to communication, being constricted in our throat and neck area can affect our ability to speak up for ourselves. Without clear energy flow in this area, we may be stifled from expressing ourselves and allowing our voices to be heard.

---

[13] Hanna, *Somatics*, p 20-21

While these body maps can be helpful for understanding the functions of our entire being, what if we took a broader perspective? What if we saw ourselves as little "earth ecosystems" and as microcosms of the entire planet?

Here is a short experiment you can try to see if you can sense yourself as a tiny fractal of the earth and as connected internally and externally. I call this "zooming" in and out.

Focus your attention on your feet to start. If you cannot sense them while still, you may need to wiggle your toes or roll your ankles around. Now zoom back out and feel the entire "container" of your body resting in awareness of itself. Then bring attention to your hands. Again, if it's difficult to sense them while still, feel free to move your fingers and roll your wrists. Really allow yourself to feel what's inside there once you are still again. Come back out to your whole body again, resting in awareness.

What if you zoom out a little further? Can you sense the space directly around your body? If not, that's okay. Consider the temperature of the air, any scents in the room, whether you are in a still place or feel any wind. Come back to your body again and the space it occupies.

Can you sense how your body is connected to any other bodies in the room in which you are sitting? Maybe you notice your cat napping on the couch. Can you sense any peaceful energy that seems to reside within or around the cat? Or if it's feeding time, maybe you sense the impatience that you haven't yet acted on their demand? Come back to your body and center yourself again. If you live with someone else, try this with your roommate or your family member.

You may start to sense the energetic connections you have with those you love. You can pull them closer in your mind and send them even more love if you wish. Or if they have done something that you find disagreeable, as happens in any relationship, you might push back energetically or shut them out. Sometimes we need to forgive ourselves for not always being as kind as we wish to be. Other times we need to suspend our judgments of others' actions. I wish I could say that is easy for me, but I am committed to ongoing practice. We get better at sensing and feeling these energies the more we practice. In Part III we will explore practical ways to do this.

Embracing What is Hidden in the Shadows

I am learning to embrace and celebrate my marginalized identities more often, and I know that others also have hidden parts. Nearly everyone has sides to themselves that they do not eagerly show to many people. Maybe you have a quirky interest in something that your friends think is silly. Or maybe you have a collection of dark jokes that you write up on your phone that you fantasize about telling at an open mike night (while you are in a witness protection program of course).

Maybe you have a gift for seeing the innocent child in everyone, that craves attention and love from a place of unhealed past trauma. You might be brought to tears by a tender exchange you see on a train or in the airport. Maybe you were taught not to show strong emotion in your family. When you do, your parents stare at you like they are not quite sure what planet you came from. Stoicism may not be accessible for you as it was for parts of your family that might have mastered it to survive. Hopefully it is not as necessary for you.

There are parts of us that sigh with relief when we come home and close the door. They are the parts that let our guard down when we relax. They are the parts that feel raw and bruised when we overshare, or when we pick a fight with our spouse for no apparent reason. There is a judge or critic within us that rejects these parts of ourselves when we say the wrong thing or were harsher with someone than we intended.

Scientists now understand that there are somatic effects of mentally berating ourselves for our less-than-perfect behavior. Our immune systems react to self-criticism by releasing cortisol, a stress hormone, and they react to self-compassion by releasing oxytocin[14]. Understanding the dialogues and stories that drive our behaviors can change the very shape and function of our bodies.

When we are going through periods of deep transformation, our brain and nervous systems literally rewire themselves. We may begin vibrating at a different frequency in our lives, feeling love, forgiveness, and joy more often. While you believe this is all good, your nervous system may resist these changes at first. We have homeostatic mechanisms in our bodies that aim to keep our internal states stable and consistent. Positive changes, while they feel good, may feel strange and out-of-place. Have you heard the expression "waiting for the other shoe to drop"? We must make room for these positive changes in somatic and energetic ways or risk self-sabotage.

Marketers exploit the fact that many of us are "on the hunt" for happiness in the form of purchased things or experiences. When it comes to joy, this is an inside job. When we feel joy and awe, we need to fully take them in. We need to be conscious and present with them to allow our nervous systems to make space and build capacity for these feelings.

Some of us mastered the art of suffering along our journey. There may not have been many people to teach us how to experience and tolerate great joy. In fact, joy is one of the most vulnerable emotions, surprisingly. To feel joy, there are elements of surrender and tenderness.

---

[14] From Kristin Neff's book *Self-Compassion*, page 165. Full citation in Notes.

For me, notions of peace and calm can be challenging to embrace and embody. For example, in every job where I master the hard tasks and things start to feel routine and easy, I get bored. When things are going well in my marriage, whether on vacation or just in terms of success we have together, I have an inner saboteur that creates unnecessary drama. This is not logical, but it points to a notion of an "upper limit[15]" that we may experience around sustaining good feelings. There may be a subconscious voice that questions if we deserve this. Or part of us may find it difficult to accept love from someone else when it is hard to feel it for ourselves.

How easily do you feel joy?

Is joy different from happiness for you? If so, how so?

---

[15] Concept described by Gay Hendricks in his book entitled *The Big Leap*.

Does it feel wrong or wicked to experience joy?

Do you ever feel guilty about feeling joyful?

The Stories We Tell Ourselves

The words we use and the stories we tell have impacts on our psyches and even on our bodies. I used to tell myself I had a high tolerance for bureaucracy and that's why I got paid the "big bucks" in the medical device industry. But was that true? In fact, I was compensated well because of the skill set I had developed over time to work with people from many different countries. My diplomacy skills were honed from years of making mistakes and learning better ways to proceed. By questioning that story, I can see that I am not necessarily "bound" to working in environments with high levels of regulation. It opens a wider range of possibilities when we consider how internal stories drive our choices.

This is the main reason why I am so committed to unpacking these stories and old identities and why I encourage you to take time for this. I can now see how I may have innocently adopted these beliefs as part of my limited view. I forgive myself for not knowing better at the time. I commit to remaining present and aware. I now make different choices that are sustainable to my spirit and support others to make more aligned choices also.

It is healthy to self-protect when we do not sense safety around us. We are socialized to present certain parts of ourselves to the world to fit into cultures. And when we come home and close the door, it is good to notice where we may sigh in relief at not having to wear the costume anymore. Assuming you arrive home to a place where you feel safe, notice what aspects get dropped. Also notice if you find yourself reaching for food or alcohol to take the edge off. You may be using substances to buffer feelings you no longer wish to tolerate, or because you have spent the day stifling what you wish you could say.

During the COVID-19 pandemic in 2020, many more of us were pushed to stay at home. Some colleagues chose not to "do their hair" or wear the high heels we were taught were proper business attire at our company. Aspects of our identities may have been liberated in some ways, and possibly curtailed in others, for those who enjoy being more social. If this was true for you, consider what parts of you might have been revealed that you want to embrace even further. A part of you may fear you cannot keep the benefits you may have discovered you love from remote working. Consider whether you can be brave and ask, "If not now, then when?"

Take a moment now to consider what "stories" you tell about your life to new people that you meet or even in your day-to-day interactions.

Are there aspects of those stories which reveal your identity and self-concept?

Are there parts of your inner identities that seem to have unfulfilled longings?

Part III – Enliven

Seven Micro-Practices – Toward Wholeness and Unity

Each of these micro-practice chapters are divided into distinct parts, including a rationale for why I include it, as well as research, and my own experiences as examples. There will be invitations to try out each practice for a week or a month to see how they land for you. There are questions for reflection as you practice, helping integrate what you are learning. A few of these chapters have guided downloadable audio bonuses that are available online so you can practice with your eyes closed, without having to hold or read the book.

Why Micro-Practices?

Now that you are aware of the importance of embracing your inner identities, and you have examined stories you are committed to unlearn that were holding you back, it is time to get practical. How do we release the old baggage to free up energy to pursue what our souls yearn for? I have experimented with many practices, especially in the past two decades, as I started truly understanding the multi-faceted aspects of my personality and identity.

Implementation is the tricky part. When you hear the word "practice," what comes to mind? For me, I remember the flute practices I endured each day starting in 5th grade with a 30-minute timer (which seemed like an eternity). I recall a couple hours of volleyball practice or track in middle school, when I signed up for what the adults told me was "good for me." Meanwhile I wished I could go home and have a snack instead. Do you recall something similar, where practice felt like a chore?

My colleague, Sam Ushio, introduced me to the term "micro-practice," and I love it. My Google search revealed that this idea is not yet in common usage. What it implies to me is that the practices I describe do not take up much time. None of the practices need to feel arduous or difficult to complete. Some of these activities can take just a few breaths or a pause of 1-2 minutes. Others might take up 10-15 minutes or more if we choose. Any of these can be practiced longer if we do have more time, perhaps on a weekend. The point is not to add more to your already busy schedule, but to free up energy for transformation.

When I do these practices regularly, they end up giving me more energy in my day, which makes up for the time I may have felt I could not spare. Once you learn them, you may be surprised to realize (as I was) that you retain better focus during the day. You may also notice that "disturbances" that might have thrown you off before are less relevant.

Self-Compassion as a Foundation

Self-compassion is a basis for all the other practices in this book. Without self-compassion, true transformation is impossible. The more we know ourselves, the more we see the shadow sides of ourselves. We might notice our mistakes and the places where we do not show up at our best. This can be painful if we are not willing to forgive the less mature versions of ourselves that did the best they could at the time.

Dr. Kristin Neff has written about self-compassion and the science and research behind its importance. Dr. Neff has some excellent free resources and an online assessment if you want to learn more about your own relationship to self-compassion. What follows in this book are my personal observations about practicing self-compassion that can get you started on this self-exploration and the personal evolution you seek. I encourage you to read her book on the topic if this is an area of struggle for you.

Experiences with Self-compassion

Self-compassion used to be quite challenging for me, and some days I still forget to practice. My fierce inner critic squawks at me when I make mistakes or do anything it deems incorrect. When I learned about the subpersonalities that arise in all people at stages of early development, I noticed these voices often sound like parental figures. Hearing my mother be merciless with her self-criticism, even though she was kind to me and rarely critical, caused me to echo her tendency toward myself. However, since self-criticism releases the stress hormone cortisol, while self-compassion releases oxytocin (the calming "cuddle" hormone), this mental dialogue has effects on our bodies. When we can notice and reframe instead of shame ourselves, we can influence the chemical cascade involved in the stress response.

How compassionate are you with yourself?

Are you able to be gentle with yourself when you make mistakes? Or do you criticize yourself?

What does your inner critic sound like?

Can you identify a voice and maybe give her (or him) a name?

Where People Get Stuck and What Can Help

People often think that practicing self-compassion means that you will lose your "edge" or your ambition. They believe that if you go easy on yourself that you will not be able to accomplish things in your life. In fact, self-compassion is what allows you to keep showing up and working toward your goals. It allows you to be brave and courageous and to be kind to yourself when you fail occasionally. If you are living a life that fulfills your deepest desires, you will experience failures along the way or things that don't go according to plan. You may even fail publicly. It is self-compassion which allows you to keep going in the face of these setbacks.

The micro-practices in this section are not a prescription for what you must do. They are personal menu of practices that help grow your capacity to know yourself and to adapt, evolve, and respond to an ever-changing world. Once you have tried them out for at least a few weeks each, you can keep what feels most helpful and discard anything that doesn't resonate. They may not all feel "easy" at first, if they are new to you, but as you practice, you will start to notice energetically which are most generative.

My suggestion is that you read through all the practices first and then pick one to start that feels easiest for you. Practice it daily, or a few times a week, for a month. If you love it and keep gaining benefit, keep doing it. If it just doesn't work for you, don't worry about it. Move on to the next or modify it to suit you. Then layer on the next practice, rather than trying to take on many at once. We are individuals with different histories and different needs. But if there's something that really rubs you the wrong way, you might inquire within yourself further to see what it's bringing up for you. As I alluded to earlier, sometimes facing the places we are most resistant to change leads to exponential growth.

Micro-Practice 1 – Journaling or Thought Downloads

Why Journaling?

There are many reasons writing down our thoughts is a foundational practice when we are diving deeply into identity questions. First, we record and make sense of the stories we are telling in our lives. Then we intentionally examine the impact of these stories in our lives. Another reason is that by taking those thoughts out of our head and moving them onto a page through our hands, we help ourselves get some distance from them. These thoughts are not who we are. These ruminations are not what will happen, but projections of our own mind. These regrets may have been about events in the past, and not this present moment.

For me, there is a real sense of "cleansing" when I take just 5-10 minutes to air out my thoughts on a page. This can be via a keyboard or by hand, whatever you are more likely to do. It can also be via voice memo if you do not like writing or have any insecurity about that process. I will explain different ways to do this in the invitation section of this chapter.

Experiences with Journaling

My experiences with journaling have shown me how important it is for me to stay in touch with what I am thinking and feeling, especially when I am undergoing a big transition in career or relationships. When I spent some time studying and analyzing my journals in recent years, I noticed something striking. During the times when I was journaling regularly, I stayed more balanced and relatively sane in my life, even if I was going through difficult circumstances.

During the times when I was going through depression, I could not find any journal pages. Part of me wonders if I threw away those journal pages, though I suspect that I had fallen away from the practice at that time. I probably told myself a story that I was too busy or that I didn't have time, or that it was self-indulgent. Looking back, I see how that vital practice allowed me to stay in touch with myself regularly. Instead of being drawn to constantly serve the needs of others, like my first husband or work and community responsibilities, journaling helped me stay anchored in what I needed. When I skipped it, I suffered and was less present in my life.

Now I use journaling as a daily touchstone for myself. I enjoy my morning pages, which I write in the first 10-15 minutes after my morning meditation. I allow whatever thoughts enter my head to pour out through my hand on a page. I use some lovely "flowy" ink to make it a pleasant tactile experience. I typically alternate colors for each new day—blue or black, and sometimes purple.

Occasionally I miss a day, or do these pages on a lunch hour instead, if I have early morning meetings. There are no rules when it comes to this practice. However, I notice that if I skip days, it is a huge relief when I return to it. I see that little issues seem to accumulate and build up when I am not releasing those thoughts on a regular basis. The "sludge" seems to build up in my brain when I don't clear it out at least every other day.

Last year my coach got me to try a new form of journaling, by recording a brief voice memo daily. I have been enjoying that as well. I still do my "morning pages" and it has not replaced this practice for me. However, if the idea of writing makes you feel self-conscious, the voice memo journal is a brilliant way to use technology to facilitate your thought download process. The added benefit of this audio journal is that you will hear your own voice and possibly be even more aware of the "tone" of your words. You can start to hear the energy behind certain thoughts and ideas. For me, I notice when I am particularly excited about a project or idea. While writing this book, my audio journal revealed when certain concepts especially resonated or when I felt particularly moved to talk about certain stories or experiences.

Processing your ideas while talking them through can be a tremendous benefit. I also find I am more scattered with this method of journaling than when I capture words by writing. It is part of the way I think and process, and there's no judgment attached. If you are new to journaling and this feels difficult in any way, experiment with either method to see what is easiest for you.

Your Invitation to the Thought Download

If journaling is already your friend, perhaps you do this daily or maybe a couple of times a week. If you don't enjoy writing, use your voice recorder on your phone and speak out loud to express what you're thinking.

This is just for you, not for anyone else.

You can use a single sheet of paper to do this. No need to have a fancy journal. You can shred it or rip it up later. No need to be precious about it or keep it unless you want to refer to it later.

Doing a thought download or a journal entry is a wonderful practice, especially for when you feel overwhelmed or anxious. When my thoughts race around in my brain, I can really start to feel the stress bunch up my shoulders or tighten my chest. Taking just 5-10 minutes to write down what we are thinking can take the "charge" out of it. We might look over those thoughts and conclude: No WONDER I'm anxious! We might benefit from naming the emotions coming up either on the page or while reading back over what we wrote. Writing can slow down our emotional processing just long enough to give us clarity and to consider how to respond.

If you are not sure how to begin, try this prompt: **what am I thinking about right now?** Or ask yourself: **what's causing the distress, love?** In this prompt, you are speaking kindly to yourself as you might to a good friend. Then let your pen move across the page without editing, without stopping and without distraction for at least five minutes.

Your emotions will come and go, and typically take about 90 seconds to process as long as we do not resist them or feed them with additional stories[16]. I will cover emotions and energy in greater depth in the fourth micro-practice. And at the end of a few minutes of writing and reflection, you may already feel calmer. If these are uncomfortable thoughts and you want to send them on their way, a ritual of physically tearing them up and throwing them away might feel good.

For people who like to make a list of things bothering them or things they fear they will forget to do (a related practice that can help especially for ADHD folks), now at least there's a list of what's looping. We can either decide to put these items into our calendar, or do them right away if we have time, or maybe delete or consciously let them go if they are not things WE have to do.

Now take a deep breath.

Don't you feel better already?

If you are feeling particularly excited or happy, this is also a great time to journal. In fact, recording those times when you feel tremendous gratitude, or you just accomplished something are also important. I often forget to take the time for that. However, there is good evidence for taking time at the end of the day to list 2-3 things we were able to get done and to take a moment to celebrate and acknowledge those things.

---

[16] From neuroscientist Jill Bolte Taylor's book *My Stroke of Insight.*

Reflection on Journaling

I hope you will practice for a few minutes each day to see if it has the impact on your life that it has had for me and for many others. Here are a couple of reflection questions to spend time thinking or writing about after you have given this practice a try for a while. Ask yourself:

How is this going for me?

What works well? Scheduling, time of day, format, frequency, etc.

What does not work as well?

How might I change it or make it easier to do?

Do I want to keep doing this? Why or why not?

Where People Get Stuck and What Can Help

If you find it hard to start this regular thought download or journaling process daily, be kind to yourself. When I went to yoga school a couple years ago, many of my yoga sisters shared reasons that journaling was difficult for them. Some associated the writing process with times in school when they felt they could not "measure up" in some way. This was especially true for those with different thinking styles or focus issues. Others felt that there was a lot of pressure if they wrote in a journal and could not do the practice every day. They preferred not to add any pressure, so filling a single sheet of paper three or four times a week felt liberating. A couple of them shared that they did not want to keep a journal because someone had read their journal and they felt violated by this. I surely would NOT want that for me or for you!

If you do not have a place where you can keep a private journal, remember you can shred the sheets when you're done. Or if you feel pressure that your writing has to be perfect, please reassure yourself that's not the case. Nobody will publish this stuff (unless you want to use this to guide your memoir someday). This is for your self-awareness and your self-study. This micro-practice is about processing, not producing.

There is no need to worry about grammar or punctuation. Some people think better in pictures. While I am not one of those, my point is to **do what works for you**. If you cannot do this daily, can you manage it 2-3 times a week instead? You might try scheduling a reminder on days when your calendar is lighter. And forgive yourself when you do not get to it.

This practice can help your own self-discovery and internal inquiry process to come to know and appreciate yourself, and to access deep wisdom. If it supports you in that, please continue with it as you layer on the other micro-practices. If it feels burdensome, move on to the next practice, and perhaps someday, if the spirit moves you, give it another try.

If you are using the excuse, "I don't have time," consider what that means. Are you giving generously to yourself as you give to others in your life? Have you been taught that it is not appropriate to take care of yourself and your needs? If these thoughts or beliefs are in coming up, how might you challenge yourself to reconsider whether those beliefs are serving you?

Caring for yourself well helps you care for the people you love. And realize that while women especially can absorb a message of "selfless service" to guide our lives, it might help to use a metaphor to remind us of why this is important. Imagine an empty cup, a beautiful chalice or just a common drinking glass from your kitchen. Now try to pour out to others from it while it is dry. Now imagine a very full cup (perhaps overflowing) and feel how eager you are to share from that abundant source. As you give generous attention to your needs, the cup fills and you give from a more sustainable source.

Micro-Practice 2 – Breathing or Breath Meditation

Experiences with Breathing

When people first started telling me to breathe, I felt annoyed. As someone with a sensitive nervous system, I can inadvertently "wind up" my own anxiety by breathing shallowly and quickly while thoughts spin. It can be irritating to hear someone tell me to take a deep breath. The problem is that so many of us have forgotten what we knew as babies, to take in a very full and complete breath and then to completely exhale and let it go.

We may not even notice when we are holding our breath. Often when we yawn it is not about being tired. It may be about allowing our bodies to take in more oxygen, and we have unconscious somatic inclinations that help us do that. If you ever feel anxious or, like me, you spend time worrying or ruminating about the future, see if you can bring your attention to your breath by bringing a hand to your belly to feel two or three nice deep breaths in and out.

Why Breathing?

Consider the origins of the word spirit or inspiration. Many ancient cultures felt that the breath was our very spirit and essence. Indeed, the first thing we do as humans when we are born is to inhale. The last thing we do before we die is to exhale. The breath is one of the few bodily functions that is both automatic and controllable. We do not have to think about the breath. Yet, when we do consciously change it, we tap into the control center of our nervous system in a profound way.

In yoga school, breath awareness is one of the fundamental concepts we learn first. It is the basis for almost all other physical and meditative practices. Unfortunately, many of us have learned "chest breathing" due to habitual sitting patterns and other cultural norms. When someone tells us to breathe, we move our shoulders and chest rather than using the full capacity of our lungs and into our diaphragm by taking a breath that expands the belly.

Donna Farhi, a movement therapist and yoga teacher, explains in *The Breathing Book* that we feel bad to look good. We have myths in our culture about how our bodies are supposed to look. For many of us, opening and expanding our bellies for a nice full breath is not what we were taught to do. We believe that holding in the abdominals makes them stronger. This is not true. Worse, it is the opposite of true. Holding in our abs in a constant state of contraction causes them to weaken. Farhi tells us that, "in order for any muscle to function effectively it has to completely relax between contractions" (p. 39).

When I feel myself holding in my belly, straining myself to "look better," I gently remind myself that I will feel better and perform more effectively with full breaths. It is a habit I am still unwinding. Please return to self-compassion if you carry any shame or old ideas about this.

Noticing our breathing and regularly taking time to observe it can allow us to show up with presence, courage, and equanimity. In the brave arena where we may unveil our hidden identities in new ways, breathing meditations help us remain centered and grounded in the validity of our voices and perspectives. While it may seem too simple or basic to make an impact, I am reminded again and again how this fundamental practice can be forgotten by our busy minds.

Your Invitation to Breathe

I will guide you here through a couple of my favorite breath practices so that you can see which ones float your boat. I encourage you to vary up your practice a bit, to see how seated versus lying down or standing up might feel while practicing. There are also breathing practices you can do while walking or even running, counting three breaths in and two breaths out. If you want more personalized guidance, apps like Insight Timer contain guided breathwork for purposes like increasing clarity or calm presence.

You may want to read the instructions out loud for yourself in a voice recorder. This is so you can close your eyes and just listen to focus more fully on sensations of breath without reading. My suggestion is that you read these instructions and then use recorded audio as a way of anchoring this breath practice. After a few times, you will be able to guide yourself through the practices. Having your eyes closed during the practice allows you to be less distracted by visual stimuli, which typically dominate our brain's visual cortex.

The most basic practice is that of **awareness:** whatever position you are in, take 60-90 seconds right now just to notice your breath. Close your eyes and just notice:

What is the quality of your breath?

What is the depth? Deep or shallow? Somewhere in between?

How fast or slow is it?

What is the texture? Rough or smooth? Somewhere in between?

Do you sense any colors while you breathe? If so, take note.

Every now and then I sense a color or even a clear bright light as I breathe. If I am feeling fatigued, my breath can sound loud, feel labored, or even "soupy" in texture. No judgment here. Our thoughts and imaginations sometimes flutter toward other things. If that happens, just notice, and come back to the sensations.

As you breathe, you may or may not notice that it automatically slows down. For me, this is almost always the case. When I bring my consciousness to my breath, it begins to slow down and even out. If you are tired or feeling down, your breath might feel heavy or shaky. If your throat feels constricted while you breath, sometimes a gentle hand resting just above your collarbones can feel soothing and supportive.

No judgement. Only noticing.

Reflection on Breathing

Once you have had time to practice these breathing invitations, I invite you to reflect on your experiences. If you are still journaling, you can write for a few minutes on the topic. And if not, then just reflect on the following questions.

What happens when you notice your breath?

Where and when do you notice that you struggle to get your breath?

Are there times when you are more aware? Less aware?

Do you feel you have to "hold in" your belly to make sure you don't look fat?

How does it feel to let it all hang out?

Where People Get Stuck and What Can Help

Truly the most difficult part of this practice is that people forget to intentionally practice. Please forgive yourself for this. I am a yoga teacher and even I forget to breathe now and then. We are called to teach those things we most desire to master. By writing this micro-practice, I reinforce a solid reminder to rejoin that daily breathing practice, even if for only three minutes a day to return to center.

I often place my hand at my belly to remind myself to take in deep breaths when I am feeling agitated or triggered. Aligning in this way can help you get back into your body and into the present moment. If we are unconscious of our holding patterns (and most of us are), then we will need to create reminders for ourselves. We can put a Post-it Note on our monitor, or even one on the fridge, or in the pantry if that is a place where we go instead of remembering to breathe.

Micro-Practice 3 – Somatic Awareness and Bodyful Practice

Why Somatic Awareness?

Embodiment and somatic awareness practices help us tune into our full experience of being human. We are sensing, feeling beings, not just mammals that think. Our soma encompasses a wider array of consciousness than just our thinking brain as I described earlier. As an organism, we sense and perceive so much more than just what our mind can tell us. I have begun thinking of the soma as an extended "root" system, like a brain that is distributed throughout our entire body. Indeed, our entire nervous system can sense the outside of us through our feeling sense. We sense where we are in space using proprioception. We sense inside of us using interoception. We know when we are hungry or thirsty because of internal signals. We know we are lonely when we feel some heartache or sadness.

Feelings and sensations give us a wider array of information that we have sadly been taught to ignore in postmodern society, especially in a capitalist, "always on," culture. Even the mindfulness movement, in my opinion, has done a disservice by putting the mind at the top of a false hierarchy. What if we lived in a more "bodyful" culture that understood that we are fully alive in all parts of ourselves, not just in our minds but in our very BEING?

In a capitalist patriarchy it is no accident that we often find ourselves cut off from our bodies in real and metaphorical ways. This is disempowering and it allows us to live in ways that are misaligned rather than harmonious with the earth. We must question who is served by these modes of disconnection. Certainly not ourselves or our communities.

Experiences with Somatic Awareness

My own journey around somatic awareness involves struggles around body image and food. While this feels vulnerable to write about, my first experiences in therapy in college were to address my struggles with depression and using food as a numbing tactic and a way to calm anxiety. I believed the false notion that girls and women who were thin and small were somehow "better" than me. I thought they were superior and had self-control. My body did not match the ideal. A misogynist culture that disempowers women fuels the tendency to judge our appearance as a worthiness marker. Many of us have started to question and decondition these culturally programmed ideas[17].

If you relate to a struggle of body image shame, it will help to approach these practices gently and with tenderness. There may be parts of your body and your soma that feel numb and difficult to fully sense and perceive. That is okay. That is a normal part of this journey. It may reflect trauma that you have experienced, either personal or collective, especially as a woman in this culture. As you "wake up" some of these parts, you may feel emotions of anger, sadness, grief, or even unexpected joy and pleasure. Allow yourself to experience these practices with a spirit of curiosity and openness and go at your own pace.

Your Invitation to Somatic Awareness

I am including the text of key practices here so that you can get started with the basics. I recommend you listen to my recorded audio version (via SoundCloud) as you first practice, so you are guided and do not have to think through any sequences. Closing your eyes will help you sense internally

---

[17] Please see Sonya Renee Taylor's excellent book *The Body Is Not an Apology* for more.

without the distraction of visual processing. I include three "levels" of somatic awareness practice because everyone is on a different place in their journey.

If these ideas are new to you, start with the beginning path and work your way into the other levels only when you feel totally comfortable practicing on a regular basis. If you are an experienced yoga practitioner, or you dance, or do other "bodyful" movement practices, you may want to move past the beginner levels into the intermediate or advanced practices.

I will admit that some days, even though I am a certified and registered yoga teacher, my body calls me to return to the beginning. This is especially true if I have been "tuning out" the body for a while or have been indulging in old habits that disconnect me from my body. I gently invite myself to return with self-compassion and curiosity. The more we practice, the more we realize that there are no real "levels," and that we can make our way back to the source of our internal wisdom with ever more ease and freedom.

Beginning – Sensing, Feeling, and Noticing

Go to a comfortable place like your bed or stretch out on the floor on a yoga mat or blanket. I like to use effortless rest position with my feet flat on the floor and my knees either hip distance apart or falling inward if this feels like less work. Close your eyes if this feels comfortable and safe, or keep them open in a soft, unfocused gaze if you prefer.

Take some time to tune into your breath as we did in the last practice. Bring one hand to the belly and one to the chest so you can feel the shape the breath makes through your body. Sense and feel this shape. Breathe a few more times while you notice this expansion and contraction as you breathe.

Now turn your attention to your entire body resting on the floor. If there is any tension in your body, notice it without judgment. Your mind may want to tell stories like, "Wow, my lower back is so stiff," or "This feels boring," or something else. That is fine and normal. Just let these thoughts drift through your mind and pass through you.

If you feel nothing or cannot sense anything yet just stay patient and stay open with yourself. Our bodies have ways of protecting us when sensations or memories are too overwhelming. One way is by tuning down the signal. If we have experienced physical or psychological trauma, our bodies may have done this naturally to protect us. They may need more time to wake up more slowly or with more support from a licensed practitioner.

Take a moment to direct your awareness to your hands. If you'd like, move your hands around, maybe flex your wrists or rub your hands together to generate some warmth. Then place your hands anywhere on your body that might like some support or attention. Using your intuition as a guide, this might be your heart, your hips, maybe even your shoulders, your neck, or your face.

As you rest in this position, notice the feeling and the energy in your hands. Allow yourself to receive this energy in any area of the body you have chosen for now. Your hands contain an abundance of nerve endings that can help you wake up parts of the body that are not as readily accessible if they have been ignored. Or if you prefer just to lay your arms comfortably to the side, notice the circulation and flow of energy through your hands by themselves.

Intermediate – Body Scan

Go to a comfortable place like your bed or stretch out on the floor on a yoga mat or blanket. I like to use effortless rest position with my feet flat on the floor and my knees either hip distance apart or falling inward if this feels like less work.

If you prefer to be seated instead, choose a position where you can remain relaxed and relatively still and comfortable for at least 10-15 minutes. Close your eyes if this feels comfortable or keep them open in a soft gaze if you prefer.

Take some time to tune into your breath as we did in the last practice. Bring one hand to the belly and one to the chest so you can feel the shape the breath makes through your body. Sense and feel this shape. Breathe a few more times while you notice this expansion and contraction as you breathe.

Now turn your attention to your entire body resting on the floor. If there is any tension in your body, notice it without judgment. As we tune into the sensations and feelings, we will work our way through a full scan, starting with our toes and feet and resting in awareness for a few moments before moving onto the next part. You may keep your body still, or if you feel an impulse to move to help you better sense your body (like your feet), you can move your toes or roll your ankles to "wake up" the part.

As you come out of this body scan practice you may feel like making some movements again to reactivate the sense of your body as a whole. Allow yourself to carry this bodyful awareness into other activities of your day. Take a 10-20 second pause in moments of the activities you do in your day to sense and feel and notice what is happening in your body.

Advanced – Taking These Practices "Off the Mat"

Now that you have begun to sense, feel, and notice the sensations and dynamic flow throughout your body while lying down or while seated, you can take this practice out into your daily activities. While you are standing, moving, or sitting, you can take ten or twenty seconds just to notice inner and outer sensations. While using a hand for any area such as the heart, belly, or throat, that needs support, you can check in with your "body compass" during any task where you feel you need internal guidance.

This micro-practice may not seem radical at first, but after I began a regular practice of bodyfulness, I could more easily feel when my shoulders were tightening in response to my thoughts. Or if I had an interaction with a person that was uncomfortable, I could feel the pit of my stomach contracting or my chest tightening.

Notice when your body wants to expand or contract in response to either a thought or a situation or a person with whom you are interacting. Notice how places and spaces affect your body. What spaces feel great to you? Are there spaces that feel constricting or dark?

Reflection on Somatic Awareness

As you begin practicing greater somatic awareness, you may find that old stories and patterns rise to the surface for your awareness. You might ask yourself these questions in your journal after a practice or write here:

What is my body telling me?

Where am I feeling expansive? Is there anywhere that I feel tension or contraction?

Where can I continue to release tension or contraction?

Is there something I am afraid to know?

How can I be of even more support to my body and my soma while I continue to show up courageously in my life?

Where People Get Stuck and What Can Help

When we have past trauma or old beliefs "lodged" in our bodies, sometimes there are parts that feel frozen or numb. This is our body's way of protecting us from old memories or traumas that we might not be ready to process without professional support. If you suspect that something painful wants to be released but that your body does not feel safe or secure during any of these practices, don't be afraid to seek professionals to support you. Nobody was meant to carry trauma alone. There are somatic therapists and other professionals who are trained to guide you through intense emotions where you may benefit from further support.

Please take these physical practices at your own pace. For some, there can be an immediate dislodging of old energy or stuck areas that feels liberating and exhilarating. For others, this process can feel slow, and it can release buried pain. The biggest thing to keep in mind is that when you practice regularly with gentle self-compassion and a spirit of openness and curiosity, you may even heal hurt places in you without having to "open up" the old stories. For those of us who have told and retold stories to a therapist, working through the body instead (or in addition) can feel liberating and a bit miraculous. We do not actually have to re-traumatize ourselves by digging into the old hurts again.

If stories surface that cause an emotional reaction, realize that some of these may not even be "yours" in the sense that they happened directly to you. I have found that my body needed to release collective grief of stories I may have taken on from friends or even yoga sisters. Ancestral trauma can come up that was passed down through epigenetic inheritance.

I was very surprised to be brought to tears during one soma yoga session in which we worked with hips. My body released deep grief at all the ways in which women have unconsciously hidden any parts of us that were seen as "too sexual." While a traumatic event may have been part of my adolescent experience, I had no specific memory that surfaced. A deep and cleansing cry allowed me to release and heal some part of me that told me I was bad or wrong to move my hips in a certain way. I sensed it was a deeper release of culturally held stories, not even my own, that I needed to release. If you find yourself crying or feeling emotional, please know that this can indicate deep healing within you. It may be just the release your body needs to invite in greater joy and fulfillment. Have compassion for that part of you that knows at a deeper level exactly what you need, even if there are no words to adequately express this felt sense.

Micro-Practice 4 – Sensing Emotions and Energy

Why Emotions and Energy?

Emotions are the energetic language that our bodies use to tell us important information. One of my favorite podcasters (Brooke Castillo) likes to explain that emotions are vibrations in the body. Another way to think about emotions is that they are energy in motion. In my yoga experiences and training I noticed that usually an emotion can pass through my body in about a minute or ninety seconds. For more "activated" states of grief or anger, sometimes emotions pass in waves or larger intervals.

Emotional awareness and fluency are skills that will become increasingly important to thrive in this changing world. Sadly, my generation learned almost nothing about them in school. For me it was not until college when I began to truly understand the impact of pushing them away rather than processing them, especially after I went through my first official depression during my senior year.

Our emotions, both positive and negative, carry a "charge" in our bodies. Consider for a moment how excited you feel when you are working on a project or participating in a cause that you are motivated to join. Contrast this with a project that you feel you "must" do but is not something that moves you. Even the language I use as I imagine these scenarios changes. Excitement creates energy. A sense of obligation feels like effort and perhaps like drudgery.

In cognitive psychology there is a well-accepted model that helps us to understand how thoughts create emotions, and emotions translate into actions (or non-action). These actions subsequently determine our results. I have included a graphic below so you can see that it is not a linear model, but rather one that contains positive or negative feedback loops depending on the thought/feeling combinations we generate to drive our actions and ultimately our results.

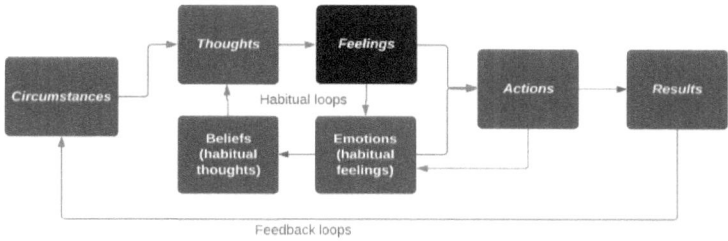

Emotions provide the energy or fuel for the actions we take. Thus, it is important to develop an understanding of our own emotional vocabulary and feeling states to help us feel less "stuck" when it comes to expressing ourselves and embracing our identities. People with ADHD like me tend to be driven by impulses and strong emotions that can feel disproportionate. Tapping into the energy of those emotions and questioning the thoughts that caused those energetic ripples can be very empowering.

Experiences with Emotions and Energy

My relationship to emotions is heightened by my wiring, which gives me greater sensitivity than the average person. This can be a gift, but it is often characterized externally as a fault. "You're too sensitive!" is what we are told. It is not a personal fault, but rather an experience of emotions that are deeply felt and a biochemical pre-disposition. We often feel deep empathy for colleagues, clients, family, friends, and even people with whom we disagree. Unless they are yelling at us. Then all bets are off, and our inner warriors go into battle. When we use these gifts with discernment, they can feel like our superpowers.

To work skillfully with our emotions is not something most of us are taught in a traditional public-school curriculum. However, in workplaces and in the public sphere we have seen examples of how this skill is increasingly important to learn. Emotions used in the service of recruiting support for an important cause, such as persuading neighbors to wear masks to protect their community, can have life-saving implications. When we tune into our empathy and see others as linked to us in common humanity, we are more likely to create rather than destroy.

When humans are under what seems like a "spell" of hatred or mistrust or racism, we may behave in ways that do not reflect our best. These behaviors are driven by strong emotions often based on deeply held beliefs. They are exacerbated by those that prey upon fears and insecurities. This is one reason why mastering our emotional states is not optional, but rather required learning for our evolution individually and collectively.

Grounding in somatic awareness is important before exploring emotions and energy because **feelings are experienced through the body.** When we feel or sense our bodies, we can discern the emotional energy that passes through us. Being able to pinpoint and describe our emotions in detail as we experience them can help us remove the charge and thus process the emotions rather than avoiding them. I truly wish I had learned this as an adolescent, since I know it would have resulted in so much less suffering in my twenties and thirties.

For people with VAST/ADHD wiring, we are motivated best by positive emotions. At the same time, anyone can be drawn into negative emotions and negative thought loops. In fact, our brains have an automatic negativity bias. What kept us safe and surviving during our early evolution was the ability to detect danger. We also had the ability to seek pleasure and comfort (food and shelter) but noticing danger is what kept us alive.

Our brain has not yet evolved to accept the abundance that exists around us. Knowing this, we can be less harsh with ourselves when our brain defaults to negative thinking. Developing ways to interrupt negative thought loops can help us stay on track with achieving our goals and heart's intentions.

Invitation to Emotions and Energy Practices

For these practices I invite you to keep your journal handy. If you have been working with the daily thought downloads, these practices will be easy to implement. If that is not yet a part of your daily routine, no problem. You can work with recorded voice memos or other body integration practices as well to help you process emotions.

One of my favorite practices is to simply locate emotions in my body. You can tune in and become aware of which parts of your body are stimulated when you experience an emotion. The observations of your thoughts while you note the sensations in your body can help you recognize how your own thoughts create ripples of emotions that have bodily impact.

For this micro-practice, allow your body to settle in an easy seated or lying down position, whatever feels most comfortable to you. If it feels safe to close your eyes, please do so, or allow yourself to have a soft gaze in front of you. Take a few deep breaths. If it helps you to bring your hand to your belly for a few moments, do this to bring awareness to your body and breath.

Scenario #1

Now recall an image, person, or place that brings you comfort or peace. This might include imagining a place in your home where you feel at ease, or it might be a place in nature. For some, there are trees or green spaces. For others there are bodies of water or mountains. Wherever you are in your mind, allow yourself to soak in the positive experience of peace and relaxation, and perhaps joy for at least sixty seconds. Then tune into your body.

Where do you experience any emotions related to these images?

Are there specific sensations you can name?

Do you feel warmth or expansive sensations in your heart?

Are there colors? Any temperatures you notice?

Are there other places where you can feel sensations?

Take a few moments to let yourself sense any bodily sensations and feelings associated with the peaceful place in your visualization. You might zoom in to locations in your body where you feel most activated. Then you might zoom out to your whole body resting in a larger awareness. Rest here for as long as you like and soak up feelings of wellbeing which you need not put into words.

The next place or situation may be a bit more difficult to experience, and I promise not to keep you there for long. Please know that in the next practice, you may return at any time to this first place if anything feels too overwhelming or distressing. Do your best to stay with the discomfort if you can and observe sensations while there.

Scenario #2

Recall a person, place, or situation which causes you to feel negative emotion, perhaps some disturbance. This is not the most difficult situation in your life, but perhaps something that causes minor annoyance, sadness, or anger. Allow yourself to take a few breaths while you experience the feelings in your body.

Where do you experience these emotions?

Do you feel them in your heart or chest area? How would you describe them?

What about your gut? Are the feelings steady, or do they change?

Any colors or temperatures present?

Are there other places where you can feel it?

Take a few moments to sense your body's reaction to this place or situation and your feelings associated with it. You might zoom in to places where you feel the most activated.

Then you might zoom out to your whole body resting in a larger context.

Sense and feel these emotions flowing within you. Notice how they change and perhaps come in waves. Now feel the safety of your body connected where you are sitting or lying and to the earth through gentle gravity. Allow yourself to come back to the present by moving or shaking out any energy that might still relate to that second memory or situation. If it feels nourishing to return to the first scenario to experience the peace and contentment you may have experienced before, allow yourself to go there.

Now move side to side, or backward and forward, to feel where your glutes and "sit bones" contact the chair, or the floor, or wherever you are, and open your eyes. Look around the room and name at least three colors of objects where you are, helping to ground you back into the present.

Reflection on Emotions and Energy

Using your journal, a sheet of paper, or this book, explore the following:

What did you notice about moving from the positive to the negative scenario?

Where did you feel the most "charge" in the positive scenario?

Where did you feel the most "charge" in the negative scenario?

Did you feel resistance to imagining the negative scenario? Where did you notice this resistance in your body?

Where People Get Stuck and What Can Help

When I first began practicing emotional awareness, I enjoyed the positive visualizations. I felt as though the tour through the negative place was not a place I wanted to be, and I noticed myself trying to "escape" mentally. My body would brace itself, constrict, and rebel. I would crave ice cream or chocolate. And when I began practicing more, I noticed that I could allow the energy to pass through my body while breathing deeply without getting "caught" by the memories or the stories that the emotions would bring up. This was not immediate, however.

Our minds can be caught up in what feels like a cascade of emotions and thoughts, each looping around each other in a way that feels pretty darn crappy. But you might also see how processing that emotion, feeling its journey through our body, and then choosing to come back to our body and the present embodied experience can interrupt the negative thought loop. Each time you feel the urge to flee from any situation where you experience discomfort, start to recognize where our emotional energy is linked to this impulse. You can allow space to make a choice about how you want to respond rather than being "ruled" by the emotion itself.

I don't mind sounding like a broken record when you read or hear this advice many times: **Please approach these practices with self-compassion and love for yourself.** If you cannot tolerate the difficult emotions at first for very long, understand that all humans typically want to press the "exit button." Observe your tendency to escape and run. Almost all of us have habit energies that nudge us to cling to the first scenario and run from the second. This is human nature. Even enlightened masters talk about the afflictions that can trap their minds temporarily. Be gentle with yourself. By practicing these observations, you are strengthening your recognition "muscles." You can also better empathize with others as you see how easy it is to be drawn into whatever stories have reinforced themselves into beliefs.

A brief distinction between discomfort and pain should be noted here. Pain can come up in emotional and physical ways, and sometimes processing old hurts or trauma will bring up intense discomfort. However, we should not be afraid to experience this if we are well supported. While pain can be an indicator that deeper physical issues need addressing, discomfort will not hurt us. It is learning to tolerate our discomfort that will let us grow into the fullness of our contributions, and beyond the limiting beliefs that may hold us hostage.

Micro-Practice 5 – Time in Nature

Why Time in Nature?

When we intentionally connect with the elements of nature, we recognize truths about our nature as humans. Particularly when we step outside the doors of our human-built homes, we encounter a world of sensation. We might feel the wind through our hair or the rain or snow on our skin. We hear a symphony of sound that is different from the sounds inside of our home. Depending on where we live, we might also hear city noise, cars, and the bustle of other people. However, something inside us seems to awaken when we leave the shelter and comfort of our homes and enter a wider connection with the outer world.

By truly connecting with nature, noticing it, and staying aware of our sensations as we connect, we recognize a part of ourselves, because we are part of nature. Despite the false duality of "man-made" versus natural objects, we begin to see the connection between what we make and the wider world around us. What we create is not (necessarily) in opposition to nature, and it is connected to our surroundings. Our creations carry elements of our human desires for comfort, ease, and pleasure. They may hint at our cravings for adventure, our discomfort with boredom, and our interest in novelty. Our possessions also signal status and identity in outer ways. By taking a step away from those items now and then, we come to understand their role in our lives while heightening our sensory awareness, which can become dull and sluggish when we are too sheltered.

Experiences with Nature

This micro-practice is a nice complement to the first four, and it can be combined with any of those practices as well. I often take my journal to a nearby park when the weather is good, so I can get fresh air while writing. In the summer after COVID-19 lockdowns pushed so many of us back into our homes, I offered an outdoor yoga class where my students delighted in watching the trees and listening to the wind during savasana (final resting pose). It was surprising how practicing outside, when most of us were used to indoor practices, felt expansive and integrative. Our nervous systems seemed to reset themselves.

Typically, I get outside at least once or twice a day for a walk, run, or errands. If you can walk for at least a mile or maybe even three, it is beneficial to your mental and physical health. Even five minutes outside, allowing your senses to take in what is around you, is helpful for your body and mind. I have known people who seem afraid of the outdoors, as though they will be harmed by it. Maybe they have learned to fear insects, allergens, or harsh weather. Listen, I also avoid getting out in sleet storms because I don't like being wet and cold. When the temperatures fall below zero Fahrenheit here in Minnesota, I'm not the first to cheer for heading outside. However, deprivation from natural light, air, and attunement with the elements leads to a dullness of the senses and stagnation internally. Even when the cold is bitter or the summer heat feels oppressive, try to spend a few minutes outside each day.

Your Invitation to Connect to Nature
What is your relationship to the great outdoors? Do you welcome the opportunity to head outside for a walk or do you procrastinate before even going out to check the mail? Maybe you have already experienced how much of a difference it makes to your mood to get outdoors, especially if you have a job which requires multiple hours at a desk during the day. Or

maybe during the pandemic you experienced less outdoor time because you didn't need to commute back and forth to an office.

This micro-practice is about consciously and deliberately using your somatic awareness, sensing, and noticing while you are outdoors. To do this, you will use each of your five senses and tune in for a few seconds or a minute for each one. Look around you and notice the colors of your surroundings and their shapes. Allow yourself to truly hear the soundscape, both those sounds near you and the ones that might be in the distance. Notice the sensations on your skin. Is the air warm, cold, cool, something else (more descriptive)? Take a deep breath and notice the scents. Absorb the obvious ones, and the more subtle ones. No need to name each one (that's the mind talking) but just come back to the direct sensations and be aware of your experience. If you can taste what is on your tongue at the time you are outdoors, this can be interesting. Perhaps you just drank your coffee and so there is residual bitterness there. Or maybe you just finished dinner and your tastebuds are sensing something else. Can you taste the crispness of the outdoor air? Spend a few minutes on this practice, or longer if you have time. If you want to layer on some elements of somatic awareness like the body scan discussed earlier, this can be a lovely form of outdoor meditation.

Where People Get Stuck and What Can Help

For most of us, what gets in the way of this practice is the illusion that we do not have enough time for it. Another huge factor is our discomfort with the weather which we may not find agreeable. If you don't want to get outside because it's too hot, too cold, or too rainy, allow yourself to feel and notice this resistance. Have self-compassion for your desire for comfort and the avoidance of unpleasant sensations. If it is very hot outside, you may need to move very slowly, or avoid walking until early morning or late in the evening. If it is very cold outside, you may need to wear some layers. Does that feel like too much of a pain to you? Some days it might feel harder to take this time. Try to get your outside gear on anyway, and head out for just a few minutes. Overcoming that initial resistance by taking a few small actions in the direction we want to go yields such positive benefits.

If you have a physical challenge that makes it more difficult to get outside, can you open a window instead for a few minutes? Or can you sit near a window so you can observe the outside? If you truly cannot get out, my coach introduced me to a practice of "elemental stillness" that can offer restoration when getting outdoors is not an option.

Here is how Stephanie Lindloff of **Our Natural Wisdom** describes it in her newsletter:

Recognize when you're interacting with one of the four Elements: Earth. Air. Fire. Water.

Pause for a sacred moment to connect with that Element.

Breathe.

Open your heart to receive any intuitive guidance.

Breathe and be present.

End by giving thanks to the Element.

Stephanie originated this practice at a time when she was somewhat housebound after the birth of her son. Rather than feeling trapped by not being able to get outside, she noticed a slight breeze causing movement of the mobile over her son's nursing chair. She was guided intuitively to notice the other elements of Water, Fire, and Earth as they were with her in the room also.

For you, the Fire might include light coming through the window from the sun. The Earth might include a wooden chair in the room. Your surroundings contain parts of all four Elements. By taking a few moments to notice all four Elements, we ground ourselves through our senses and re-establish our connection with Mother Earth. I found this to be incredibly helpful, as have many other clients she has mentored.

Reflections on Time in Nature

After you have had time to get outside for a walk or just for a few minutes of breathing, ask yourself a few questions and write in a journal if you choose:

What senses felt most active and alert today?

Are there any insights I received while connecting with Elements of nature?

How might I carry forward this sense of connection into the rest of my day?

Micro-Practice 6 – Creative Expression

Why Creative Expression?

Creativity is one of the most joyful parts of being human. It is a nourishing wellspring of delight and play. It is a place where we may lose track of time, though that doesn't always mean it is easy. Some creative endeavors involve cognitively challenging effort. However, most of us experience this type of challenge as deeply satisfying. When we neglect our creativity for too long, Brené Brown says that "it metastasizes[18]." When I first heard that, of course I thought about cancer and how it spreads. When we hold back our creative impulses, they tend to come out in unhealthy ways.

Creativity is fundamental to identity because it is this self-expression that allows us the freedom to be who we are, and to meet our inner worlds. And while we are not our "art" alone, it can be a vehicle to express our deepest joys, sorrows, and desires for the world. But before we get to the invitation, I want to dispel a few myths about creativity. We often think of it as a practice we learn in art classes, or maybe in writing or in music. Creativity goes far beyond this. It can extend into collaborative processes like leadership and into other activities like group facilitation or organizing a movement.

Your creativity might be the simple act of moving through your morning with intention and presence. Every day you create your own experience by showing up and deciding how you will participate and respond to life. Even times when you think you are not being creative, you are always authoring your life and writing your story. We have more control over our inner experiences of life than we realize. This is where

---

[18] From the *Magic Lessons* podcast with Elizabeth Gilbert, Season 1, Episode 12, July 25, 2016.

creativity can help us to break out of those limited ways we have learned to think or the old paradigms of who we are.

Maslow's hierarchy of needs puts aesthetic and self-actualization needs in later stages of development. But he also wrote about exceptions to the model, including his puzzlement over the "creative artist.[19]" Our needs for safety and belonging are rooted in acceptance of who we are fundamentally. I realize that an understanding of neurodiversity and hyper-focus were not as well understood during the early days of humanistic psychology. Experience has taught me that our self-expression and creativity are deeply embedded into this divine part of us, our very soul.

When we imagine divine mystery, we are often beckoned toward forces outside of us. Indeed, the earth from whence we came is the ultimate Creatrix, making up our very essence. And at the same time, we exist in constant co-creation with her, playing ourselves into existence in an ongoing relationship. Looking within us is perhaps the greatest and most worthwhile mystery we will ever contemplate.

Experiences with Creativity

What I love most about creativity is that it as a constant flow throughout our lives. Creativity is a choice, and a way of being and living. While it may only trickle on some days and it might appear in a raging waterfall on others, it will always be there. Even in times when we are not "producing" as much in terms of writing, or speaking, or outward expressions, our conscious and subconscious awareness always plays with what we receive. When we give ourselves time each day or each week without the distraction of too many outside inputs like podcasts or television, we may delight in playing and coming up with new ideas and possibilities. And sometimes our inner

[19] https://www.td.org/insights/maslows-hierarchy-separating-fact-from-fiction

divine takes on new challenges in a subconscious way that is mysterious and may seem illogical to an outside observer. They seem illogical to an inside observer also!

Back in 2017 when I was anticipating my second marriage, I had a strong urge to start my first blog, www.meximinnesotana.com. While I was not sure what this project would ultimately mean for me, I knew it had emerged partly as a search for personal identity outside of what it meant to be a wife again. Perhaps part of me felt confined in claiming that label and craved a different way to express myself, my virtual soapbox to channel whatever needed to come through. Blogs are a beautifully open medium. I used mine to restore my "roots" of a regular writing practice in a more public way, something that I had done before only in journals for private purposes.

At first the blog was something I did a few times a week. I soon realized how much I loved the practice. On days when I wrote for 20-30 minutes before work, I felt energized and happy. On days when I did not "have time" for this practice, the day seemed to drag by at work. At one point I decided I would post daily for a month. This rapidly grew to many months in a row. Then for one year, I had posted for 356 out of 365 days. Those of us with ADHD are often criticized for inconsistency. I had worked my way out of that old "inconsistent" identity into a new concept of myself: brave experimenter. What parts of your identity might reframe themselves in a new light when you give them air and space through creativity?

Your creativity is for you, not necessarily for other people. You can share what you create when you opt to do so. Other times it may have therapeutic benefit in allowing you to play with new ways of being. When you explore thoughts, feelings, and intentions, sometimes being your own audience is enough. If you know you will have to share, you might censor yourself in subtle ways. To allow for deep truths to emerge, Virginia Woolf taught us that a room of our own may be required. I deeply concur.

Your Invitation to Creativity

For your initial invitation to creativity, feel free to dip your toes or fingers into several different "media." If your first impulse is to write, go for it. But if you have already been doing that while reading this book, you might try something new and different. If a birthday is coming up, decorate a cake. Draw a scene on a sketch pad or paint a room of your home (while using plenty of drop cloths of course). And allow your body to source aspects of creativity that you may not have embraced before. You might dance to a song you like or take a Nia class online, in a costume.

These acts of creative impulse have no rules. But if you can, it might be generative to allow your body to be in motion. Much as I love writing, there is not much motion beyond my fingers, and my hands raking through my hair as I try to find the right words. I often need to prepare for my writing in a physical way. I may do a couple of "plank" poses to activate my solar plexus while I'm on a writing break. Bodyful yoga can warm up and flex the parts of my body that have not been in motion during longer writing sessions. Sun Salutations can feel good, or even a downward dog. Opening the blood flow and prana (energy) can facilitate our creative flow. Tea or coffee might help wake up your brain if you feel sluggish before entering the zone.

What little ritual might give you the nudge to get you started? Can you make your creative session a sacred act by lighting a candle or playing some lovely music? Do you like gazing at a favorite bookshelf or looking out the window for inspiration? Go where you are moved to begin, and if you need to set an alarm to get to work on time, please do. I've been known to lose hours in creative flow, and if this is a possible "hazard" for you, take steps to be a responsible adult, if you must.

I will refrain from giving specific instructions on this practice. If you have experimented with the previous practices, your body will know intuitively what to try first. Staying open to at least three or four different "modes" of creativity may open others. Remain open to what arises. If you have ten minutes to engage in your private creativity practice, do it! If a weekly session for an hour or two on a Sunday morning is more to your liking, do that instead.

For some of us, our workplaces allow for creativity every day. If you are in a position where that is welcome, feel free to implement your play time at work. It may surprise you what you are able to create when you free up the different modes in this space. If you can engage a colleague or two in mutual creativity on a project excites you, this can be the juiciest place of collaboration. And if this is not possible for you right now, no worries. There are many other times in your day when you can free your muse and allow her to play.

Reflections on Creativity

As you practice creativity on a daily or multi-weekly basis, ask yourself the following questions in your journal or via voice recording:

How did it feel?

Are there places where my creativity is overflowing into other areas in my life?

How can I let creativity flow into my relationships? Work? Hobbies?

Is there anything emerging from my creative space that scares me?

Are there places I am holding back?

What expectations do I have of my creativity?

How can I allow myself to play freely without attaching to any particular result?

Where People Get Stuck and What Can Help

The biggest places where people get stuck with creativity practice is thinking it needs to look or sound a certain way. Many creative processes are not neat and tidy. We need to feel comfortable to make a mess if that's required. Throw paint onto a canvas, and drip things onto the floor. Allow ink to spill out and for words to be misspelled. Take that knitted hat and miss a stitch here or there. Allow it all to be gloriously imperfect and unprescribed.

The perfectionism monster can lurk when we are creating something new that we don't yet understand. Unfortunately, this can stop the flow of true creativity when we attach too much importance to one session or creation. Sometimes we may feel an impulse to destroy a creation. To me, when you do this, you've truly arrived. You know there's more where that came from, and you don't need to grip any of it too tightly.

Maybe you think you do not deserve the pleasure of creativity and aimless play for your own sake. Archeologists have unearthed objects of beauty that were made not simply as utilitarian objects, but also adorned with decoration. No permission must be granted to have the right or privilege to create. While many of us have jobs and families to attend, we can always find a way.

If creating a meal from the ingredients in your kitchen feels like a sacred act to you, this is creativity. If mending a shirt or sewing a button goes beyond a chore and allows you to flow with your creatrix energy, embrace it. Sometimes tiny acts can be approached with a spirit of creativity, regardless of the time you have. Do not allow your busy schedule to be an excuse for tamping down your creative urges.

Micro-practice 7 - Dancing with Life and Finding Our Rhythms

Why Dance?

I introduce this practice last because I spent thirty years of my life neglecting it, not that it is less important or significant. In my forties I returned to dance by taking classes with my favorite yoga teacher. I now attend Nia classes with Beth Giles as often as I can to move my body with joy and freedom. After decades of body shame and feeling like I was "too fat" or too awkward or too clumsy to dance in public, I have let go of those stories.

Dance allows us to find and reconnect with the rhythms within our bodies. Some of us dance quite freely. Others of us have had to overcome feeling shame about moving our bodies in certain ways that draw too much attention to ourselves. When we were children, most of us moved quite naturally when we heard music. Somewhere along the way, if our bodies did not conform to the beauty standards we were taught to envy, we may have lost the desire to dance.

I introduced somatic awareness early in the micro-practices because reconnecting with our bodies is fundamental to reuniting our full consciousness of being. Bodyful practices are sorely needed, especially in a world that has disconnected with the body of our earth. While stillness and meditation are important practices, giving equal weight to movement can help us move stuck energy through and outside of us. Many of us spend a lot of time sitting at jobs in front of computers. This creates bottlenecks in our circulation and the flow of energy through us. Dancing can be a way to release and channel healthy energy through the body so that we can experience all that is meant for us.

Invitation to Dance

Do you dance already? If so, this practice may be easy for you. Just be sure to spend some time each week moving your body in a joyful way, whether you take a class or just put the music on. If you do not dance right now, and you prefer to move joyfully in another way, through running or playing a sport, this is also wonderful. Have compassion for yourself if this practice feels vulnerable. It took several years of dedicated yoga practice for me to feel comfortable enough to restart my relationship with dance. If the usual definition of dance is not physically accessible to you, can you move your body within your imagination? Matthew Sanford, a yoga innovator, explains that the places we don't feel are still graceful.[20] The compassion we feel for those parts that work to keep us living can heal a deeper layer of ourselves.

You might start with just moving to music, which is free and doesn't require a class. You can watch dance videos to get your inspiration going if that feels fun to you. If you want to connect with one of the online Nia classes that I love so much, look up Beth Giles on Facebook, or email me at cristy@wedefydefinition.com so I can share her latest newsletter with links to classes.

---

[20] From podcast *Becoming Wise* with Krista Tippett, "Matthew Sanford: Compassion for our Bodies," April 4, 2016.

Reflections on Dancing

As you dance or afterward, consider the following questions:

Where do you feel most free in your body while you dance?

Do you enjoy dancing alone or is it more fun to dance with others?

Do you feel any restrictions while you dance? Where? Are there stories that arise?

Does anything feel released when you dance?

Can you be goofy and silly when you dance?

Can you remember the childlike bliss of moving without being self-conscious about others' attention?

Where People Get Stuck and What Can Help

A few years ago, at the age of forty-four, I overcame three decades of body shame to dance again. My former yoga teacher offered a dance foundations class that helped me re-engage. I allowed myself to be an uncoordinated beginner at this practice. After so many years of telling people, "I don't dance," it took some time to unwind the identity of non-dancer or "awkward mover." When my hubby jokes about my "white girl dance," I just laugh at him now and tell him he is jealous of my moves.

Many of us feel vulnerable when we dance. Our parts may move, jiggle, and bounce when we dance. This is a beautiful thing. I still judge my body now and then when it doesn't look the way I want it to look while dancing. This is an ongoing journey. However, when I focus purely on the joy of moving my body rather than worrying about how I look, this feels best. I was relieved when I could dance online during COVID-19 lockdowns. Previously we danced with mirrors in a studio. While this can help some people in aligning with a teacher, for me it was a judgment minefield.

In this "new world" of technology-assisted gathering, maybe we can allow for more ways that people of all abilities can move and dance without the self-consciousness. With our cameras off and maybe in our pjs after a rough night, music and dance can transform our moods in ways nothing else can.

Part IV – Evolve

Shifts That Occur as You Reshape Yourself – Inside & Out

If you have begun to practice the suggested ideas in this book on a regular basis, you may already notice shifts occurring within you. If you have read the book and intend to go back and explore later, you may have questions or resistance toward beginning. Some of your past identities or subpersonalities may rise to protest: "This is too much work!" All ages and stages of your experience are alive within you. They do not leave just because you have reshaped yourself. The idea is not to banish them or to ignore what these parts have to say. Like toddlers, these parts tend to get louder when they are ignored.

You may need to consider how to comfort these developmental parts of yourself that served you well during earlier life stages with different conditions. Speaking to these parts kindly and in a reassuring manner may seem soft or silly to you. Yet you know it hasn't worked to chastise them or treat them unkindly. Consider how you would treat a beloved pet that occasionally comes toward you with an exuberant rush at an inopportune moment. Might it be more effective to calmly express love toward that being rather than harshness? As your nervous system calmly responds to the interruption, you calm the creature within also.

As you continue to change shape in the way you relate to the world and to your colorful cast of inner identities, your outer landscape may change as well. Friends who were part of your "old life" may drop away. They may not feel that they recognize you or that you have much in common anymore. You may even find that some family members look at you as though you've just arrived from Mars. Are you the same person they raised? Their faces may register confusion and shock at times that you have become more truthful about things they prefer not to discuss. This can be difficult to accept at first. Those internal changes are taking on a new and different shape that may not feel quite like your own for a while, like a borrowed pair of jeans. And for those that are not witnessing your transformation from within your soma, they may wonder silently, or out loud, if you've lost your mind.

In one sense, you have lost your old mind. Your "new mind" has begun to experience itself in a more loving and liberating way. You have moved beyond the old neurobiology that had grooved itself deeply and subconsciously into the person you used to be. That may feel strange and different at times. You may experience what sociologist and life coach Martha Beck calls "change-back attacks" in which you find yourself reverting to the old patterns to return to the familiarity of what you once knew. This is normal. Nothing has gone wrong. You can stand your sacred ground again when you have centered yourself back into peaceful and calm space of your Higher Self again.

As others sense the energy and aliveness that you feel, some will be jealous. Many will be suspicious. Your partner may even accuse you of having an affair as you will be lit up from within in a way they may not have experienced before. Some people may be resentful. They may not like the boundaries you have created to respect the ebbs and flows of your energy. Perhaps this means they have had to learn how to do things that you used to do for them. While some may respond with interest and increased confidence as you have delegated responsibilities, others will push back. This is fine. You understand this is not about you, and you treat these reactions with compassion and love.

Scaffolding Through Community Supports Change

While you navigate your new path, you may find it helpful to find community in new ways with others that are also experiencing this accelerated growth. Even if we unite with others on very different paths, you sense there is a commitment to live differently than the unconscious ways that a consumer-oriented culture has reinforced. You will likely find yourself developing your own daily practices beyond the ones suggested here. Feeling drawn to gather with others who are reshaping themselves and reshaping the world around them is a natural part of your journey. It is not necessary to completely leave behind family and old friends. However, we must become more discerning of effects of our interactions on our energy and spirit as we learn to build healthy boundaries.

One gift of the COVID-19 pandemic was that many of us who had felt trapped into spending time in ways we might not have chosen now had an opportunity to reconsider. Many of us were grateful to catch up with people we missed and wanted to hug again. What a joy to reconnect. We also realized how much we appreciated the newfound time and lack of pressure to be social as often as others may have wanted.

You may need to be more selective about how you spend your time. This disruption provided a liminal space that many of us needed to question our patterns of over-extension. We may have learned to take a pause before engaging in old habits. And while some will return to similar work or habits we had before, the texture and flavor of our days has been forever altered.

In Closing – A Benediction

Let us now choose the canvas on which we will paint our future and invite collaborators who energize and hold us during this transformation. Let us appreciate that in each moment we choose how we respond to our reality. We shape our futures through consciously choosing thoughts that lead to the emotions that fuel actions for a healthier planet and more sustainable lives.

As we connect with somatic healing deep within ourselves, let us pour our flowing abundance of energy to those around us. As our contributions flow into the collective energy, let us receive wisdom on what needs to be healed further. As we move beyond what we have known before, let us be grateful for new awareness. We release the breath we have held. Tension dissolves away for a few moments. The earth releases her abundance. We gratefully receive. We consider what next steps best suit the moment and act skillfully and with love.

Connect

I hope you receive my words with curiosity, amusement, and recognition. Your personal journey will look, feel, and sound different from mine. You are a multifaceted and beautiful human. I hope you appreciate and celebrate this regularly.

As you experiment with the micro-practices in this book, I encourage you to stay in touch via my website. The audio file for the guided somatic awareness practice can be accessed via SoundCloud. This book shares my present knowledge on what works for me and for many of my clients. I am constantly exploring and discovering ways to dig deeper and to live with greater joy and freedom. I write blogs and share other content on these topics which you can find at my website listed on the back cover or on my YouTube channel.

If the concepts in this book resonate with you, and you want further support, I am honored to share mini-courses and guided meditations with you when you feel ready to delve in further.

I also lead interactive workshops for companies looking to sustainably build more inclusion into their cultures, and I speak about these topics also. We all yearn to bring our whole and integrated selves into our work. By engaging in our personal explorations of identity we honor ourselves. By nurturing ourselves well, we serve the evolving needs of our workplaces, and we create more sustainable futures for people and for the planet. We unite our collective strengths and create the scaffolding for more engagement and fulfilling work. Be well.

Acknowledgements

This book could not have been written without the support of many people. Thank you to my dear coach Stephanie Lindloff at Our Natural Wisdom for being an early believer in this project. I am deeply grateful for your steadfast dedication to helping me overcome personal obstacles to getting this done. Kay Grey, your astute editing work helped me spare my readers and clients from wandering too far off track. Thanks for being willing to work with me.

Heather, I just love the original art you made for this book, and I'm so grateful for our weekly soma yoga sessions. Natalya, thanks for championing in this project and creating a cover that I'm excited to share with readers. Joshua, your 30-day book challenge kicked this off. Though I ditched my first draft after 4 months, knowing I could draft quickly gave me the confidence to start over and hire a professional editor for the part where I struggle most.

Thank you to my friends and colleagues who are learning to love and accept their neurodiversity, and bi-cultural Latina *mujeres* in my life whose faces appeared before me as I wrote. You provided the emotional fuel and drive to complete this project. To my clients and friends who have shared parts of their personal journeys with me, *mil gracias*. Thank you for encouraging and supporting me to keep going on this project. I am eager to keep doing our brave work as we celebrate our wins together.

Deep gratitude to friends who agreed to read parts of the book along the way: Thomas, Claudia, Oscar, Jane, Kathleen, and my Puttyverse friends. Your willingness to offer your impressions kept me clarifying my ideas when I was at that vulnerable stage of sharing. To Terry, Dale, and Julie: You are superstars! Reading the manuscript when I was too bleary eyed to edit anymore felt like absolute grace and relief to me. Jeanne Felfe, kind mentoring on formatting the book for Ingram saved me from throwing in the towel on the paperback. Julie Davis, thank you for your guest room and the company of your dear kitties as we embarked on the challenge of editing my longest writing project to date. Your thorough review of the manuscript helped me focus and refine my ideas.

There are so many authors I wish to thank for the ongoing inspiration and encouragement, even though they have never personally met me. Martha Beck, Elizabeth Gilbert, Brené Brown, Sonya Renee Taylor, Glennon Doyle, Lisa Espinosa, Austin Channing Brown, Louise Erdrich, Orna Ross, Jenny Blake, Emilie Wapnick, Roxanne Gay, Resmaa Menakem, Thomas Hanna, Christine Caldwell, Emily & Amelia Nagoski, Scott Eblin, Celeste Ng, Don Miguel Ruiz, Dani Shapiro, and Erica Sanchez: you are among the author/mentors I see on my shelves each day. Thank you for being my teachers without even knowing the influence you have had on me personally.

A deep bow and thank you to my family of origin, Christine, José, and Wendy. You provided me with such love and care to set me up for success in my life. I am so grateful for all of it. Thank you to my chosen family also. This includes my running community, yoga teachers, and all friends who helped me during our pandemic year(s) to stay focused on the vital things. I love you and hope you call on me when you need me.

To my husband Clem, you make me a better human being by reminding me not to take myself so seriously. At least not ALL the time. Thank you for making me laugh and for being my partner in so many adventures, including a global pandemic. I look forward to going out, having new adventures soon. I can't wait until we can return to Canada to do the Superior Circle Tour in the opposite direction next time.

End Notes and References

Beck, Martha. Finding Your Own North Star: Claiming the Life You Were Meant to Live. New York, Three Rivers Press, 2001.

Beck, Martha. The Way of Integrity: Finding the Path to Your True Self. New York, Penguin Life, 2021.

Brown, Brené. The Gifts of Imperfection: Let Go of Who You Think You're Supposed to Be and Embrace Who You Are. Center City, Hazelden, 2010.

Caldwell, Christine. Bodyfulness: Somatic Practices for Presence, Empowerment, and Waking Up in This Life. Boulder, Shambhala, 2018.

Channing Brown, Austin. I'm Still Here: Black Dignity in a World Made for Whiteness. New York, Penguin Random House, 2018.

Dispenza, Joe. Breaking the Habit of Being Yourself. Carlsbad, Hay House, 2012.

Doyle, Glennon. Untamed. New York, Penguin Random House, 2020.

Eblin, Scott. Overworked and Overwhelmed: The Mindfulness Alternative. Hoboken, John Wiley & Sons, 2014.

Haines, Staci. The Politics of Trauma: Somatics, Healing and Social Justice. Berkeley, North Atlantic Books, 2019. Audiobook.

Hanna, Thomas. Somatics: Reawakening the Mind's Control of Movement, Flexibility, and Health. Cambridge, De Capo Press, 1988.

Hendricks, Gay. The Big Leap: Conquer Your Hidden Fear and Take Life to the Next Level. New York, HarperCollins, 2009.

Huber, Cheri. Making a Change for Good: A Guide to Compassionate Self-Discipline. Boulder, Shambhala, 2007.

Menakem, Resmaa. My Grandmother's Hands: Racialized Trauma and the Pathway to Mending Our Hearts and Bodies. Las Vegas, Central Recovery Press, 2017.

Nerenberg, Jenara. Divergent Mind: Thriving in a World That Wasn't Designed for You. New York, Harper Collins, 2021.

Neff, Kristin D. Self-Compassion: The Proven Power of Being Kind to Yourself. New York, HarperCollins, 2011.

Strozzi-Heckler, Richard. The Art of Somatic Coaching. Berkeley, North Atlantic Books, 2014.

Taylor, Sonya Renee. The Body is Not an Apology: The Power of Radical Self-Love. Oakland, Berrett-Koehler Publishers, 2018.

Yoshino, Kenji. Uncovering Your Authentic Self at Work. LinkedIn Learning, August 18, 2021.

Thank you for supporting this indie author's first book!

We Would Love Your Feedback

Review Request

If you received wisdom and value from this book, would you consider leaving a short review on your favorite online bookstore that takes reviews?

A good review is important to indie authors these days as it helps other readers know if this book is a valuable use of their time. It doesn't have to be long or detailed. Just a sentence saying what you enjoyed, and a star rating would be fabulous.

Many thanks.

www.ingramcontent.com/pod-product-compliance
Lightning Source LLC
Chambersburg PA
CBHW020358130626
46549CB00006B/2330